Lickskillet
Revisited Julius Cord

and Other Stories

Lickskillet Revisited

Published by

Julius Cord
4453 Oaklawn Drive
Okemos, MI 48864-2921

Library of Congress Control Number: 2008936793

ISBN 978-1-60702-804-8

Cover illustration by Gary Montgomery

Table of Contents

Dedicated to

George Edward Cord

Duck Hunter Extraordinaire

My brother George was an out-of-doors person as were both his father and his paternal grandfather, both of whom spent most of their working lives on the Missouri River. His maternal grandfather made the long covered-wagon trip west to the state of Washington twice.

George grew up in an era where there was an abundance of migratory waterfowl. This eventually declined into a daily limit of one or two birds of selected species. He maintained his hunting habits throughout this slack time and kept his same routine with blind building, the placement of decoys, and time spent in the blind, hoping that a small flock or single local duck would appear in his binoculars as he scanned the northern sky.

George hunted ducks in the traditional way, no doubt practiced by his father and grandfathers. He found some slack river water, dug a hole for the blind in the river bank, cut willow saplings that he placed in front of the hole, and put the hand-carved wooden decoys in the shallow water in front of it. Then he sat in the blind and waited.

He kept this routine for more than forty years, except for his military time. I guess it proves that the "hunt" is the thing, and the shooting at ducks was a small part of the total hunting experience.

He had a natural flair with the duck call, of which he had many, and he could almost talk the duck's language. I have seen him talk to a departing flock of ducks in their hurry to go south and actually have them turn around to get another look at his decoy setup. Sometimes all it would take is a single duck to flare to one side and come by, and the rest of the flock would follow him. I have not seen that many duck callers, but George was by far the best caller in our group.

Duck hunters are like golf players who get a new model set of clubs each year. If one of George's many hunter friends had discovered a new and much better duck call, it would not be long until George had it in his collection.

He also had a natural talent for wing shooting, whether or not it was a 13-ounce-weight of the migrating Green Wing Teal or a German dive bomber in World War II.

His reward? A slow, home-roasted young Mallard duck basted with honey and soy sauce for the whole family to enjoy for Sunday dinner.

Introduction:

Excerpts from the the original edition of *Lickskillet*

Sometime in the early part of the Twentieth Century the northeast corner of the city of Leavenworth, Kansas, came to be known as "Lickskillet." One would logically conclude that the people here were so poor they had to lick the skillet so as not to waste any food.

I have no idea of the original area encompassing Lickskillet. It's boundaries were generally from Ottawa Street to the military reservation and from Fifth Street to the Esplanade. I decided to write about the neighborhood I knew best, concentrating on the area north of Ottawa Street and east of Fifth Street, Fort Leavenworth on the north and the Missouri River on the east.

This is the area where I carried the morning *Kansas City Times* and the evening *Kansas City Star*, summer and winter. I did it the old fashioned way, carrying the newspapers in a cloth bag over my shoulder, papers that I folded twice and tucked one end into the other to form a throwable missile. All of this was accomplished while walking down the middle of the street. The paper was thrown on my customer's front porch. Mostly.

There are several landmarks that help define the character of Lickskillet. To the east and most imposing was the Missouri River. Next was the double set of tracks of the Missouri Pacific Railroad, and the tall grain elevator on north Main Street. Lastly, on the highest hill of the river bluff was the Old Cathedral Church with its tall bell tower at Fifth and Kiowa.

Between the river and the railroad tracks was a huge mound of mine tailings called the "Slate Pile." It extended north from Dakota Street for about a quarter of a mile and was covered with scrub trees and bushes. It was *the* place for kids to play and hide, out of hearing, from parental calls for supper.

The east side of the slate pile, next to the river, was a perfect place to pick up flat pieces of slate and see who could skip them across the surface of the river the farthest.

The slack water next to the bank and far away from the main current was the location of the old swimming hole, where generations of children learned to swim without parental interference.

Many of the men of Lickskillet worked at the now-abandoned coal mine on the northeastern edge of town. They were immigrants from Poland, Germany and Ireland. The only clue that a coal mine had formerly been there was a concrete slab over the shaft. There were also a number of soldiers living here, retired and on active duty, from the Army's Ninth and Tenth Cavalry Regiments, the black Buffalo Soldiers.

I told my two pre-teenage grand nieces that if you skipped a piece of slate across the surface of the river you will always come back. So far they haven't returned, but when they do, they will bring the beautiful children with them from Hawaii and Washington State to carry on this family tradition.

It was in Lickskillet that I was born and spent my early years. Most of the things I have written about occurred in the 1930s, told to the best of my recollection some seventy-five years after the fact. Hope you enjoy.

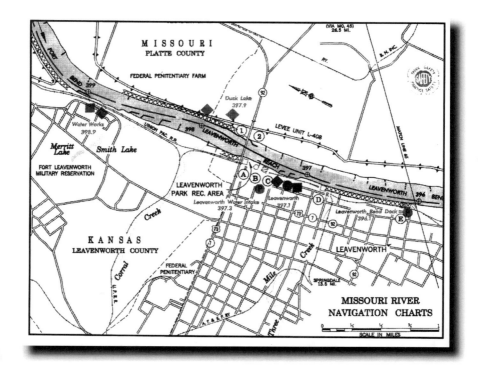

This map from an Arm Corps of Engineers Missouri River navigation chart shows the Leavenworth Bend.

Map of Lickskillet

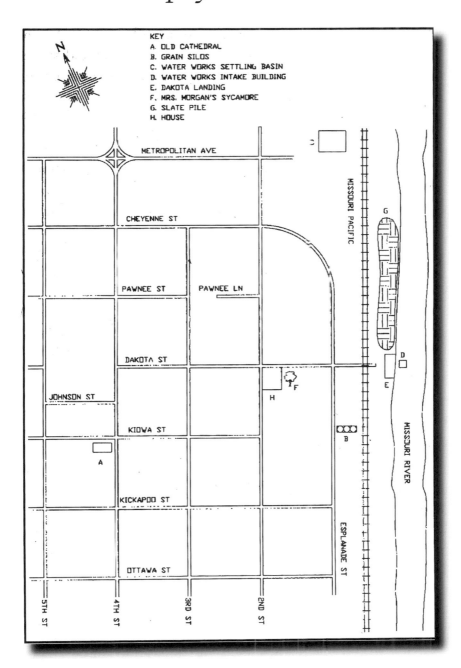

Lickskillet Revisited

When I was seeking verification on some of the things I put down in my previous book, *Lickskillet*, I called Mr. Pat Baskas, an old-time Lickskillet resident. His family's business was a tavern on the northeast corner of 4th and Pawnee Streets, and he clarified some things I was writing about. His father's name was "Sheenie" Baskas, and he had several sons, all of whom were well known about town.

So like before, when I had questions recently about something I had planned to write for this book, I again called Pat to verify information I had, as well as seeking new information. He promised to check the things out, and we ended our conversation.

Within an hour, his wife, Dorthy, also a Lickskilleter, called to tell me she had a copy of her great-grandmother's scrapbook and that I might find something interesting saved therein.

Her great-grandmother was a close neighbor when I was growing up, just across Dakota Street between Second and Main Streets, and I used to cut her grass occasionally. Their name was McKay, and Mr. McKay was a Missouri Pacific railroad employee.

The scrapbook was some two hundred pages of aged yellow newspaper clippings from Kansas City papers and the local *Leavenworth Times*. There was no backing on the book, and most of the pages were loose. Three-fourths of the pages were articles about famous movie stars, presidential photos, and current events, including Amelia Emhart, a local girl from Atchison, Kansas.

Each page of the book was completely filled with glued-down clippings on both sides, and unfortunately almost all dates were not included. As nearly as I can tell, most of the articles were published in the late 1920s and 1930s.

The remainder was a valuable collection of Lickskillet citizen's activities, including their births, marriages, deaths, troubles with the law, and whatever else she thought it would be nice to remember. Some of these stories I will write about here.

One of the things that impressed me about this scrapbook is that in my previous book, I told about things through the eyes of a five to fifteen year old boy. Whereas this scrapbook sees through the eyes of a fifty to sixty-five year old woman via the *Leavenworth Times*. There are some handwritten notes, but most are illegible.

In my first book I wrote extensively about the people, the things we did, and the Lickskillet I knew when growing up in the 1930s. One of the things I wrote about in the chapter "Street Sounds" was the blowing of the steam whistle from the mines calling the coal miners to work or to stay home. Later on, no one I knew could ever remember hearing that early morning blowing whistle. One man who lived on Billy Goat Hill, located almost over the Riverside coal mine, could not even recall the blowing.

In the scrapbook loaned to me by Mrs. Baskas I found a notice in a *Leavenworth Times* clipping that the whistle at the Home mine had blown notifying two hundred workers they had been called back to work just before Christmas. It noted in the paper that the mine had been closed since the previous May when a union agreement was reached and a strike was terminated. The warm weather reduced the need for coal for heating purposes and it stayed closed until cold weather returned in December. Leaving the family breadwinner without a job for some seven months helps you to understand the economic level of Lickskillet, and helps identify reasons for its name.

The article closed admonishing readers for not supporting the local businesses and going elsewhere for their coal purchases. Sound familiar? I have heard this spoken about downtown Leavenworth when the Plaza shopping center opened on the south edge of town. It took some businesses away and forced other local businesses to close their doors.

One of the things a lot of people did was to make their own homemade beer called "home brew." I knew of one family who made a five-gallon crock of home brew every weekend, and by the next weekend all five gallons had been consumed. There was no problem with the bottling because they were not needed. They had a ladle, and when you needed a drink you just removed the wooden lid and took as much as you wanted.

There was a family who lived two houses to the east of our home on Dakota Street named Spain. They were quite well known to me since as a precocious five year old I felt any place that did not cross Second Street was my personal domain. I visited them often and had never observed any crocks of beer. The following incident probably occurred sometime in the early 1930s, and is quoted verbatim from the *Leavenworth Times*:

> "A police raiding squad acting under orders of Chief H. T. Madison entered the home of Thomas Spain, 111 Dakota, last night at 9:30 o'clock, confiscated 52 pints and 15 quarts of home brew, and placed Spain under arrest on a charge of violating a city liquor ordinance.
>
> "Spain admitted possession of the home brew in police court this morning, but he said he did not know if it contained more than the legal amount of alcohol. He said there were eight members of the family and several of them had been in ill health and drank the homemade liquor for the tonic effect of the yeast."

The article continued with Judge T. Homer Davis deferring sentence until a chemist's analysis could be ready for presentation. I guess the judge did not buy the bit about alcohol content being low enough to be legal. I would think the color of the beer would make it easy to identify.

That reminds me of a friend who, while attending the University of Kansas, used to fly all the way to Oklahoma in an airplane owned by one of his fraternity members and bring back enough liquor to last a month or so.

This worked great until someone crashed the plane and they had to find other sources. They finally selected a farmer living about one hundred miles west of Lawrence near Junction City, Kansas.

This also worked great, and during one visit to the fraternity's favorite bootlegger they picked up the whisky and told the farmer that their guys were getting tired of the "White Lightning." They would appreciate it if the farmer could get them some real bourbon whisky on their next monthly run.

The next month the farmer produced some beautiful amber colored liquid. This pleased the driver to finally be able to bring back a load of bourbon to the fraternity house. He had visions of a long aging process in charred oaken barrels.

But when the driver drove around the house on his way out of the farmyard, he noticed an olive drab blanket draped over a clothes line with the letters "U. S. Army" stenciled on the side and a big circular white area near one corner.

They wanted color? That's what they got. But straining the whisky through the Army blanket was not exactly what they had in mind.

As I read through the scrapbook, one thing that kept coming up was about people who had died or been injured. Today, they could have been saved by modern medicine. For example, throughout the clippings were notices of persons dying of blood poisoning.

These things happened in the early 1930s before the sulfur drugs of World War II and the wide use of penicillin later on. But because I am really getting over my head when I try to talk about medicine, I will stop right here. On the other hand, here are a couple of examples of what I found in the scrapbook.

For instance, little things kept popping up reminding me of things other than drugs that we did not have in the 1930s. I will quote the headlines mostly because they are usually self-explanatory.

"John H. Thomas Dies at 21 Years of Age. Blood Poisoning From Splinter In Finger Fatal to Kaaz Manufacturing Company."
"Mrs. L. E. Taylor In Sudden Death. Loss of Blood Following Extraction of Tooth and Weak Heart Brought End Early Friday Evening. She was 25 years old."

I was surprised to find one of my grade school classmates

listed. It told of this five year old girl who had been climbing over a picket fence, fell off, and caught her little finger which was completely severed. When she left the doctor's office he told the girl she would be all right if she did not get infected.

The book listed several instances of people I knew losing infants to pneumonia. There were many cases of people dying of heart ailments and of alcoholism, and I wonder how many of these people's lives could have been saved with modern medicine.

BEGIN INQUEST INTO DEATH OF JOHNNIE LANGE

Coroner's Jury Is Hearing Evidence in Case of Man Killed by Mike Bader Here Saturday Night—Verdict Late Today.

MADE THREATENING REMARKS

Witnesses Testify That Lange Attacked Bader Without Cause, and Threatened to Kill Him—Had a Knife in First Brawl.

BULLETIN.
At 3:30 o'clock this afternoon the coroner's jury returned a verdict of "justifiable homicide," exonerating Bader. Lange met death by a gunshot wound in the hands of Mike Bader, according to the verdict, but the word "feloniously" was omitted, and under the law no responsibility can be fixed. Bader was discharged following the verdict.

There was a detailed account of two men arguing. One man had a large knife and started a fight with another man who was holding a child while sitting on a rock. The aggressor was upset because the man with the child would not fight him, and he made it clear that if he did not fight, he would kill him. And if he did not do it today, he would do it tomorrow.

The man with the child withdrew into his house and returned with a shotgun. The aggressor made threatening remarks and charged the man with the gun who shot and killed him. (Taking a knife to a gun fight? Not cool. Taking a knife to a shotgun fight? Really not cool!)

There was a story I think everybody knew about but me concerning one of the last standing landmarks in Lickskillet: The Kansas Central Elevator at Main and Kiowa Streets. This occurred one late afternoon and happened on the west side of the large grain silos.

A nineteen year old man with a history of mental illness had somehow reached the lower rung of the iron bar ladder and climbed to the top of the silos.

The man was spotted by a passing work train, and they notified the police station when they reached the local train depot.

The police then sent a motorcycle officer to investigate, and he saw the man near the top of the ladder. Since the elevator office was closed and no telephone was available, the officer had to speed some nine blocks back to the police station and notify the fire station of the need at the elevator for the ladders on a fire truck.

When the officer returned the man was not visible on the silos' ladder. He learned that while he was away the man had slipped or jumped from the top of the elevator and was killed.

This is another example of a life that might have been saved, but this was long before radios were available on police motorcycles to quickly communicate emergencies.

I was really sad to read out about the man jumping. Now when I see the silos, the first thing I think of will be the young man falling, instead of all of the good things I viewed from the top of the same silos when I had a bird's-eye view of all of Lickskillet.

A LEAP TO DEATH FROM ELEVATOR ON NORTH MAIN

Floyd R. Miller, Member of Soldiers' Home, Was Killed Instantly Monday.

WAS MENTALLY UNSOUND

Record Discloses He Enlisted in Sixth U. S. Engineers and Was Discharged From Army 2 Days After.

Floyd R. Miller, 19 years of age, leaped to his death from atop the Kansas Central elevator, Main and Kiowa streets, about 7 o'clock last night. He was killed instantly in the more than 100-foot fall.

Horrified spectators saw the youth clinging to the top-most round of the ladder. Then suddenly he seemed to loosen his hold and came hurtling down. He was dead when persons reached him.

One of the nicest presents I ever had was when I saw two men in the alley on the south side of our house on Second Street. When I asked them what they were doing, they said they were surveyors measuring the property where the half-standing "Old Brewery" building was located and that they were going to build a large swimming pool 15 or 20 feet from out property. This was to be a summer-long project, and I got to know a lot of the men and horses by name as I sat fixated in the alley or on Second Street looking through perimeter fencing.

The shape of the pool necessitated using two horses with slips and a flat bucket with handles held by a driver with the horse reins around his neck. When the slip was filled with dirt it was hauled out of the pool site, dumped, and the team would return for another bucket load. The whole project was a WPA (Works Project Administration) job sponsored by the Federal Government intended to give work to needy people. This occurred during the mid-to-late 1930s depression, and not only Lickskillet but the whole country was in dire straits.

Like most city boys, the only horses I was really acquainted with were the gallant "B-Movie" racing stallions that were always pictured with head and tail held high and a flowing mane. The horses hauling the slips though were working horses with their heads held low, mostly geldings, and some were in bad shape physically. Several had cataracts on one or both eyes and could hardly see.

Some of them had a giant sore, sometimes bloody, on their shoulder under the horse collar called fistulas. These wounds were caused by the constant rubbing and pressure from the collar. As long as the horse was wearing the collar while working there was probably not going to be much relief for the horse.

Little did I know then that I would be involved in the construction business the rest of my life, and engineering in particular. I was always enthralled in making model airplanes out of balsa strips, and when the structure was finished I never finished the planes by gluing paper on the frame work. I was satisfied in just looking at the finished structure.

Back then I think I watched most every truck that hauled the concrete to cover up the tied reinforcing metal bars in the floor of the pool, and later in the formed walls. When the structural concrete was finished I watched masons, a bit farther away, build the changing rooms and the shelter house on the south end of the pool.

Now that the pool was finished, I still had a front row seat at the deep end as I sat in our alley and watched all the colored kids swim in the new pool. I could not go to this pool, nor did I want to go there. I had the whole Missouri River as my personal swimming hole!

The name Goose Town was a familiar name to me. Like Lickskillet, it had indefinable location, and I knew it was somewhere west of Broadway and bordered Metropolitan Street to the north. I remembered Goose Town primarily because of the catchy name of their baseball team. It was called the "Goose Town Goslings."

An old friend who was raised in Goose Town told me about one of the team's very good left-handed pitchers. He had one problem, or perhaps an asset. He was "cross-eyed," and when he was pitching with a man on first, the man on first base would mistake his looking at him with the left eye and thought a "pick off" play was coming, and the man would dive back to first in time to hear the ball hit the catcher's glove.

I always wanted to know the name of the Lickskillet baseball team, but never could find it until I had my hands on the old scrapbook. A one-inch item from the *Leavenworth Times* issued this challenge: "The North End Dynamiters have confided their desire to meet the Theur Blues in a baseball game any time before the end of the season." I would assume the name Dynamiters referred to those men who worked in the old mine and used dynamite to get at the coal.

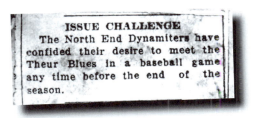

ISSUE CHALLENGE
The North End Dynamiters have confided their desire to meet the Theur Blues in a baseball game any time before the end of the season.

In retrospect, I never intended this introduction to deal so much with home-made beer or whisky, but I will write one more because of an article I found in the old scrapbook.

In my previous book I called attention to the location and demise of the local "mom and pop" grocery stores in Lickskillet. There were also as many, if not more, local saloons where you could buy beer and outlawed liquor by the glass. There were eight open bars that I know of, and that did not include the bootleggers.

There is an old-time picture of a downtown Leavenworth building that housed the "Star of the West Saloon" that was being closed down because of the noisy activities around the "Cock Fight Pit." The saloon was but one of the 120 drinking establishments then operating in Leavenworth. I am sure this was before prohibition. I am also sure that there were nearly as many or more illegal operations in the era between prohibition and the repeal of the law.

The local political party blatantly turned their head to the enforcement of the laws, and the picture in the book shows state officials closing down a "Blind Pig" and forcing the local mayor to resign. The heading on the clipping reads, "Blind Pig Receives Its Walking Orders." Although I was familiar with the term Blind Pig, I never knew exactly what it meant.

The photo shows the inside of Thomas Hogan's joint at 223 Delaware Street. The inside of the building opens to a room with no windows or doors, just a one-foot square hole, shoulder level high, where money was passed through and liquor or beer was passed out to the customer. The main purpose of the construction was to protect the bartender from identification and arrest.

It's clear I come from a family of outdoor people. When you have a family of three boys and three girls—and you all live in a living room–dining room combination and a kitchen—if anybody got too noisy or bothersome, my mother yelled scat. We were all outdoors people instantly!

The men were all hunters and fishermen. They never shot wild game except for food, and the fish were for food too. But if there were more fish than we could use for our table, there was always a market for them from the poor people. If we shot more rabbits than we needed, we could sell them to Fred Kruger's market at 4th and Kiowa for a quarter each. If the weather was cold, he would hang them in front of his store.

When you get a bunch of men together, especially hunters and fishermen, the stories just flow. Some are a little hard to believe, but most were true. Some are funny, some sad. I found that I had remembered a lot of these stories and decided to write some of them down as I remembered them, and occasionally I added a little bit of embellishment. Some of the stories are old and a some of them are within the past year. I hope you enjoy reading them as much as I did writing them down.

Part One

Lickskillet
and Other
Kansas Stories

Treed Coon

This tale occurred outside the town of Leavenworth, Kansas, during a coon hunting experience.

Two brothers were out coon hunting with their pack of hounds on a dark winter night when the weather turned warm. With high humidity and a bit of a fog the conditions were perfect for the hounds to follow the scent of a running raccoon.

It did not take long for them to pick up the scent of a coon, and after a long chase the hounds barked "treed," and the men found the dogs frantically baying around a dead tree.

When the men finally reached the dogs and shone their light up in the branches, there was no raccoon to be found. Yet the dogs would not leave the tree or quiet down, so only one solution remained. This had to be a hollow tree, and the coon had to be inside.

After spending a few minutes talking about the pros and cons of trying to get the coon out of the tree—and considering they had no outside source of income and that it was possible to hide the money they could get for the coon skin from their wives (and this time of the year the coon's fur was in prime condition and could readily be sold), and they had to have some reason to feed a pack of dogs all year long and a few dollars could be stashed away for a casino trip—they decided to climb the tree and get the coon!

One of the men climbed up the trunk of the tree with a flashlight and found the top half of the tree was broken off about fifteen feet above the ground. When he shined the light into the bottom of the hole he could see a coon there.

He asked his brother on the ground to hand up the rifle so he could shoot the coon. When he had the gun though, he found that with the precarious footing on the wet limb he was standing on he could not hold the light and shoot the gun at the same time.

Reluctantly, his brother climbed the other side of the tree, and with better footing to stand on, held the flashlight at arm's length down into the hollow tree onto the coon, and he shot the coon.

Success! Except for one thing: How were they going to get

the coon out of the tree? This is where typical American farmer ingenuity took hold. Eureka! The brother who shot the coon would climb down, go to a nearby broken-down barbed wire fence, take a long, loose piece of the wire, climb back up the tree, stick the wire down into the hole, twist it around and around so it would tangle in the coons fur, and then pull it up while the other brother held the light.

This worked like a charm, and they were congratulating themselves when the coon was being pulled out of the tree. Only one thing was amiss. There were two coons in the hole, and the coon that was pulled out was not the one that was shot, but an uninjured, fighting mad, live coon!

Let me set the action for you: Brother one, the shooter and barbed wire twister, was in a precarious position 15 feet above the ground, clinging to the wet branches of a dead hollow tree. He had barbed wire twisted around his hand, with the other end of the wire twisted into the fur of a totally upset and ready to fight live coon. The coon was growling and snarling, and trying to claw and bite anything it could reach, and all of this about a foot in front of the man's face. Brother two, the flashlight holder, was approximately the same distance away from the coon and desperately trying to protect his own body parts, while still trying to maintain his footing on the wet bark of the tree. And when he pulled his hand away from the coon, he dropped his flashlight into the hollow tree.

Now, not only do they have a problem with the coon, but it is also completely dark. Below the tree the dogs have got into a fight-killing frenzy, and anything that fell out of the tree, man or beast, was going to have a pack of wild dogs ripping into him.

Naturally, brother number one let go of the barbed wire that held the coon, lost his footing on the slippery tree, thankfully to gain a foothold halfway down it where he held on for dear life. Brother number two had a better place to stand, and he just crouched down and let all the action happen away from him at the top of the tree. They just decided to hold onto the tree until daylight, and by then maybe the dogs would recognize them and they could safely get down from the tree.

If this was a military action we would have an after-action

report, and this is what this is: The dogs finally quieted down and just moved the action away from the tree and disappeared deeper into the swamp where they picked up another coon track, and could be heard baying treed in the distance.

When the dogs quieted down, the men felt their way to the ground and searched around for the dropped rifle (which, after examining it the next morning, showed teeth marks on the wooden stock). Both agreed more hunting that night was out of the question and they left for home.

Since they were hunting on ground familiar to the hounds, they were certain the dogs would come home when they were through hunting that night. They were right, and the dogs were waiting for the brothers after their long walk back home.

This had to be one of their most exciting hunts ever. The only losses were one prime coon pelt, one five-cell flashlight, one hunting cap which the coon must have knocked off the shooter's head, and one damaged rifle stock.

No one knows what happened to the coon. He has probably become a great-grandfather by now, spending his whole life avoiding hollow trees and detesting barbed wire.

The brothers are still following coon hounds at night and telling this story to whoever will listen and enjoy.

Farm Boys

When you are raised on a farm, you grow up much faster than the kids in town. A farm boy soon learns to do the ordinary farm chores that a grown up normally would do. It is quite common for a farm boy to maintain and operate a tractor or other type of large farming machinery used in the field when he is in his early teens.

They also have time for other manly pursuits such as farm pond fishing and hunting pheasants and quail if he or his dad has a bird dog—or rabbit and squirrel hunting if he has any other kind of dog.

They also learn to be self-reliant. If they get in any physical problem, they know help is not as close as the corner drugstore; or if in serious harm, the hospital is not ten minutes away.

Most of them will try anything once, and if it goes okay they may try something again if the right conditions are present. Some of the things they attempt are unimaginable to town kids.

One of the once-in-a-lifetime things that turned into an often-repeated-event was revealed when a boy, his brother, and a good friend grew weary of trying to catch pond fish and decided to go test a backwater slough of the Missouri River. It was formed through countless floods, and when the waters receded, lots of fish were left swimming in the now landlocked water.

The brother's father was a good friend of the owner of the local hardware store who knew the boys. When they came in telling him that their dad was clearing some farm land of trees and was blowing up some stumps, they had no problem getting sticks of dynamite and dynamite caps to explode in the slough. Now all they had to do was insert the cap into the sticks of dynamite, attach a fuse, light it, and toss it out into the water. After the explosion the fish near the blast would rise to the top of the water, and all they had to do was wade out and pick up the fish. No more fishing pole, line, hooks, or bait! Fortunately, this new method of fishing produced more fish than they could eat or sell, and they finally had to give it up.

And the bait was especially bad. Here was one old-fashioned recipe aimed at that big catfish that you supposedly could not catch any other way: Get ½ pound of liver (cost: 5 cents) and two large bananas (cost: 10 cents). Dice the liver, mash the bananas, place them in a pint Ball fruit jar and tighten the lid. Place the jar in a hot place (like under the front seat of the car) and let the ingredients ferment. This concoction is best in mid-summer (*recipe from Lillard Hill, Tracy, Missouri*).

Another thing the farm kids did was to learn a lesson the first time they tried it. They went hunting rabbits with another friend who had a ferret. Now everybody knows how to hunt with a ferret. You find a hole in the ground with a lot of dirt strewn outside, and that hole is probably a rabbit warren which deserves a closer look.

First, you reach inside the ferret's cage, trying not to get bit. Then you take out the ferret and put it in the hole. The ferret runs into the hole, and you hope he does not catch anything in there that he likes to eat. Because if he does, he may be in there for quite awhile eating what he has caught and then going to sleep.

Anticipated procedure: Ferret goes in, and the rabbit comes out at rocket-propelled speed mode. Shoot rabbit. Actual happening: Rabbit comes out racing at the hunter's feet. Shoot at the rabbit. Shoot again when the rabbit is a little farther away. Missed twice. Rabbit on its way to Atchison County via Oak Mills.

Then, American farmer ingenuity: Next time out, get gunnysack. Hold over the rabbit hole. Catch rabbit in a sack. Dispatch rabbit by hand.

Actual: Sack is held too close to the hole to see what goes into sack. Rabbit goes into sack followed by ferret. Both in sack. No volunteers to put a hand in sack to grab ferret or rabbit. Dump both onto ground, and rabbit flees chased by ferret. Hunt is delayed until ferret can finally be caught.

Alternate solution required: Sack's held too close to the hole again. Turned head when distracted at the moment a rabbit hit the sack. Grab hold of rabbit in sack before ferret gets in the sack. Fold sack back, just as the rabbit miraculously turns into a beautiful black-and-white skunk starting to reinforce his olfactory reputation. Drop sack. Leave guns, sack, and all other worldly possessions, and depart in haste in the opposite direction from freed skunk, which is moving away at a leisurely pace.

26

American farmer ingenuity strikes again. Combine fishing skills with hunting skills. No, no dynamite needed this time; use a fishing dip net with holes too small to let the ferret through. Caution: If skunk is in the fishing net, be sure to flop the net open on end to let skunk escape before you leave area.

I had a good friend whose daughter married a farm boy, and they lived on a farm not too far away from her father. They soon had a baby boy who spent a lot of time with his grandfather who considered the boy the "apple of his eye."

The grandfather heard of the 4-H Clubs where a child was taught responsibility in the care of farm animals and who actually took over with the cleaning and feeding of an animal of their choice.

The animal of choice of his grandson was a baby lamb, and the ten year old boy was zealous with its treatment, and the animal continued to grow. The proud grandfather was continuously praising the boy and his lamb to anyone who would listen to him, and that included perfect and not-too-perfect strangers.

After a time, when the lamb was grown, all the local 4-H animals were to be sold at auction. The boy and the grandfather sat in the first row awaiting the auctioneer to start the bidding.

When the boy's lamb came for bidding, the grandfather was pleased to offer a nominal bid to get the bidding started. He looked at the smiling face of the little boy and was proud to continue bidding for the lamb. He did not realize though that the animal was such a grand specimen and that it would attract a highly-spirited competitive bidding from several people in the back of the room.

He looked at the boy again and decided there was no way he was going to disappoint his only grandson, and so decided to keep bidding until he was the owner of the lamb. What he did not know was that after hearing endless talk about the lamb during all of golf season, his golfing buddies showed up and they all kept bidding until finally giving in to let the grandfather buy the lamb.

When the bidding was over and the grandfather walked out of the arena with the little boy, he was stopped by the auctioneer who thanked him for the vigorous bidding. He said that he had been in the business a long time and that was the highest bid he had ever seen on a lamb!

The two, grandfather and grandson, left the arena together hand-in-hand with a tether on the lamb. The smiling boy looked up at the doting grandfather and said, "Papa, next year I am going to raise a steer!"

I am sure this kind of story has been recorded in almost every 4-H auction, but it is enjoyed more when it happens to someone you know personally.

My own personal experiences as a farm boy happened when my sister married a young farmer who at that time was working as a section-hand on the Burlington Railway. It was a job that kept him away from home for a couple of weeks at a time. Being away from home and leaving a new bride alone was not the ideal way to start a new marriage, so he quit the railroad job, and they worked a farm north of Tracy, Missouri.

Being in my early teen years and raised in the city, a chance to spend some time in the country was something I looked forward to doing. I was an eager visitor and actually went there to work with them on the farm during the summers.

The primary crop was the raising of a small acreage of tobacco. Harvesting this crop required some functions that being young with nimble fingers proved to be very valuable (such as pulling weeds out of a bed of growing tobacco plants under a thin cloth blanket, and especially planting the 8-inch tobacco plants while sitting with a companion on a tobacco setter).

The tobacco setter was a four-wheeled machine with small wheels in the front and much larger wheels in the back. The wheels in back spanned a barrel of water lying on its side with a driver's seat on top of the barrel.

In front of the barrel, sitting about six inches above the ground, was a seat either side spanning a plow making a very small furrow where the plants, held in a box on both of the planters laps, were placed in the ground one at a time. Alternatively, when the machine made a loud click, a splash of water was put in the ground at the same time a tobacco plant was put in the furrow. The boy in the right seat used his left hand for the planting, and the boy in the left seat planted with his right hand. This is a good example of a boy doing a man's job successfully.

This whole operation was propelled by a pair of mules that were walking very slowly close in front of the setter.

The operation was often in jeopardy when one of the mules would loudly expel gases literally three feet in front and just two feet above the planter's heads. This helps in understanding how some farm boys excel in profanity at an early age!

The rhythm of the planting could not be altered. If a planter was distracted and a plant was not placed on time, there would be a void where a tobacco plant should have been, and it would be obvious through all the growing season.

The last time I planted was with a neighbor we happened to visit named Bill Wills. He was a man who raised show mules and always had a team or two showing at the American Royal livestock show in Kansas City. He had a trio of young sorrel mules who seemed to think it was their job to tear down their stalls. Their kicking was very loud, and I wanted to go see them but I was too shy to ask to get a look at them.

Mr. Wills had several young men setting tobacco but needed another. Since I was available, I hired on. His farm was about a mile away, and since I had no other means of transportation, I decided to ride a very old—and very big—white horse. There was a bridle for it but no saddle, and I was told all I had to do was fill a sack with straw or hay, and the horse would be good enough for only a mile ride.

Good idea, except the big bony back separated the sack of hay in about five minutes, and my back bone was clashing with his back bone all the way to the farm.

The tobacco setting halted at quitting time, and now being an experienced horseman, I decided to ride one of the mules back to the barn. This worked fine until we came to a gate that was opened by one of the farm boys.

Now farm boys, being farm boys, could not pass up such a chance to welcome a city boy to the farm. As I sat astride my long-eared steed and passed the gate, one of the boys jabbed the flank of the mule with a hoe handle, and it made a loud snort and started crow hopping down the road.

That was my first and last crow hopping experience. The mule did not buck hard, just pranced along with short hops that proceeded to unseat me after about twenty feet. There is no way I could get off gracefully since I had no saddle, no reins, and did not know what I was doing.

The next thing I knew I was laying with my head and shoulders on the ground, and my left foot was way above my head and tangled up in the harness. When I fell, the mule stopped, turned his head around looking down at me and wondered, no doubt, what I was doing down there.

The farm boys had a laugh on me, and I thought it was funny after I was loose. I have always had a soft spot in my heart for mules since then. Had it been a horse instead of a mule, I could have been dragged all the way to the barn.

I have always heard about the intelligence of mules being greater than horses, but the only time I saw two mules with a chance to run away was when we were setting tobacco and were low on water. We pulled the tobacco setter next to an old abandoned well and stopped.

When we removed the wooden cover to the well we found it was home to two giant rattlesnakes that put up a very loud commotion, certainly rattles loud enough for the mules to hear. I do not know what a horse's reaction would have been, but the mule's only reaction was a disinterested look over their shoulders.

I was sent to the house to get a gun to use on the snakes, but by the time I returned the snakes had escaped back into the rocks around the well and were free.

There was one hill on the farm that was noted for all the rattlesnakes that lived there, and no one wanted to go to get all the squirrels that lived there. I went there often, only it was keep one eye out for snakes and one out for the squirrels.

I enjoyed working on the tobacco farm. My extreme height was beneficial in passing the just cut tobacco stalks with the leaves still attached high above my head in the tobacco barns, and I was sought after in tobacco housing time.

I liked the stripping and sorting of the leaves in the stripping rooms where the tobacco is graded by color from the best near-white tobacco near the bottom of the stalk to the dark-red near the top end of the stalk.

I now occasionally give my friends a lecture when I break open a cigarette and explain the type of tobacco therein. There are often a lot of pieces that are dark stems, and some just the sweepings off the warehouse sale barn's floor, and maybe a small leaf of near-white good tobacco from the bottom of the stalk.

I was working on the farm at a young, very impressionable age, and I often amaze some of my friends when I sound off about some of the sayings I picked up from my country associates who were mostly first- or second-generation Kentuckians. My grandfather came from Kentucky too, but that was in the 1860s.

If I am playing golf with friends and happen to describe a dry area of rough as "that ground is so poor you couldn't take five gallons of whisky and raise hell there," I have to pause and wonder where that came from. Or maybe I would describe some scantily clad young girl as "she didn't have enough clothes on to flag a hand car." They must have had railroads in Kentucky, too.

Once I heard a mother describe her thirteen-year-old daughter's flirting antics with boys as, "Don't bother with that, she is just spreading heifer dust." I did not pursue it since I was probably about thirteen too, and too shy to ask. I am still not sure what it means.

So that's my bit about farm boys. I have many friends who are farmers, especially from the town of Kickapoo that is just north of Leavenworth, and I still see them when I visit Kansas. They would take me day hunting with them just as they did many years ago. After a while, our time in the field following the pointers diminished, and we spent more time at Ma Crockets tavern on Kickapoo Road and Highway 73 playing an aggressive card game of "Pitch" than we did hunting.

They say you can never go back, but I did, and I still do.

Pheasant Hunt

November came, and it was quite a shock. It seemed like we had just started our duck hunting on the Missouri River, and now it was time to think about pheasant hunting in western Kansas.

It was a good year for ducks, and we experienced one of the biggest concentrations of them at one time, something we had not seen in years. Hunting on the opposite bank of where we had our cabin, we were in jeopardy of high wind or a fast rising river, so we had to watch the weather maps and forecasts daily.

We knew there was going to be better than average hunting one weekend when the National Weather Bureau map showed a large low-pressure area with its counter-clock-wise winds, centered in Minnesota. To the west of that was a large high pressure area located in North Dakota with its high winds blowing clock-wise.

The two rotating winds combined to give the migratory ducks a high velocity ride in what seemed like a huge funnel going right down the river and past our blind. We saw uncountable thousands of ducks going by us. The ducks were stretched out in long V's very high in the sky and far out of reach of shotgun pellets.

Our blind was dug into the east bank of the river, and we could see flocks stretching far to the western horizon. When we got into the boat to pick up downed birds, we could see the flocks stretching far to the east horizon.

Most of our shooting would normally be at small flocks, or sometimes one or two ducks. Now we were being visited by flocks of twenty or more who had been in the air for a long time and were tired and needed a rest or water.

We often had a buzzing fly-over of flocks of 100 or more ducks just looking at our decoy layout, but not getting close enough to shoot at. Usually these big flocks always landed in the river, far out of reach from our bank blinds.

Sometimes when were watching a very long V of ducks high in the sky, a little flock would break off the end of the V and come sailing down very fast to look at our decoy layout, and land nearby or out in the river.

We soon had our bag limits, and yet we stayed in the blind

most of the day in what was a bird-watchers paradise. We saw mostly Mallards, but occasionally we would be startled by a flock of fish ducks with their heavy body and rapid wing beat that sounded like a jet engine when they passed some 20 feet over our heads.

We were even privileged to see a huge flock of White Pelicans migrating. These are huge birds with a 7 foot wingspan, and if you were not familiar with the birds one would think they were snow geese. They have an unmistakable flight pattern. They fly very high and are easy to recognize once you have seen them migrating.

They fly great circles, and one would think they would never make it south, but if you turn your head for a few seconds you will be surprised to see they are gone. Sometimes they fly so high you cannot see them until they turn and the sunlight is reflected off their wings, and then they are in plain sight.

This is supposed to be a chapter about pheasant hunting, but when you give an old retired duck hunter a typewriter, and no one is around him to interrupt him, the duck stories just fly!

At this time we were pheasant hunting in northwest Kansas around the town of Norton, some 350 miles from home. We stayed at a private home and ate our meals at the local restaurants. The lady who rented us rooms also had a business of dressing out the birds for a slight charge, and that relieved us of an unpleasant chore and allowed us more time to hunt.

We were a party of four hunters and two dogs. I had my liver-and-white pointer, Nancy's Babe (her registered name), but she allowed us to call her Babe.

The other dog was a huge male Irish setter named Pager. This dog was owned by my good friend and hunting companion, Tony Oberforcher, who also drove us in his SUV-type vehicle that had a wire fence about 2 feet inside the rear door. This was an ideal place to keep the two dogs, and there were rugs on the floor to keep the dogs as comfortable as possible…and thankfully separated from the human passengers.

Our intent was to drive to Norton, check-in and secure our lodging. We were to spend the night and then drive the roads seeking someplace to hunt the next day when the hunting season opened at noon.

Everything was going as planned. We all met at Tony's house, loaded all our gear between the rear seats and the dog fence, and we were on our way.

We had not hardly got out of town when a faint smell could be noticed coming from the back of the car. The longer we drove the stronger the smell got. When finally we could not stand it any longer, something had to be done about it.

Both of these dogs were very comfortable riding in autos and had spent a lot of time riding to and from hunting trips. But what we found was that one of the dogs had diarrhea and had splattered all over the floor, and the other dog had vomited, making one smelly mess. Or, one of the dogs got car sick to start, and the other complied. Or on, and on, and on. I don't think we ever got that matter settled. The question was, who is going to clean out the back of the car?

We settled it this way. It was Tony's dog, Tony's car, and Tony's problem, Tony, with lots of sympathy—and unwanted suggestions and just a little bit of help—did a masterful job with the cleaning, and he received a standing ovation.

Tony was a very avid hunter, and a thing like a little housework did not dampen his enthusiasm for the hunt, and we were soon on our way, making it the rest of the way to Norton with the back window of the car cracked to help air out the lingering smell.

We started out in the car the next morning with the windows down, driving very slowly, looking at potential hunting sites. If we found a place that looked promising, we would stop and look it over.

The early morning was clear and cold with a heavy frost, and the brilliant sun made you think you could see forever in the flat western prairie.

We found one likely place to hunt, and we stopped to check it out. It was a north-south road, and there was a lonesome tree about 30 yards west of the road. The tree was about 15 feet tall and had lost all its leaves, and it was shaped in a perfect circle that a tree grows into when it is not hampered by other trees and is allowed to grow into its natural shape.

The land was sloped slightly away from the road, and we could hear a beagle-type dog baying maybe a couple-of-hundred yards to the west. We crossed this site off because we thought someone was probably already hunting there, or at least the dog running could make the pheasants edgy or already have flushed them away, and we left. I did not know then that this tree would provide one of my most memorable wildlife memories.

For some reason, about a half hour later we turned around and headed south down the same road. We could see the tree in the distance, and what a change had occurred.

As we neared the tree we could see it now held twelve to fifteen pheasant roosters perched and scattered throughout its branches. Everybody was aware of Christmas time, and here was a perfect nature Christmas tree.

The pheasants in their beautiful fall plumage were a joy to behold. The brilliant red on their heads and the equally brilliant blue on their necks were highlighted by the white stripe around their necks. The speckled body and long tail complemented one of nature's perfect creations.

We did not stop, but drove slowly by, leaving the sight for someone else to enjoy. No one even suggested that we stop and shoot these birds.

Later in the same day I accomplished one of my other feats that I have kept secure in my memory bank. I was following Babe because she was acting like she smelled birds, but she veered off. I saw what I thought were birds ahead, but she did not come when I called her, so I went ahead without her.

A pheasant jumped and I fired, another jumped and I fired, and another jumped and I fired. A triple? Not exactly. They jumped one at a time so it was not a true triple, but I had three birds in my hunting coat. A lot of times I have hunted all day for one bird, but having three within ten seconds was unbelievable.

After hunting ducks from a blind where the shooting is not close-in and with medium-size targets, then to go shooting quail, which is close-in shooting at very small targets that can call for very fast shooting (especially when you are in the center of a covey and they all flush at once), when you shoot at pheasants over a pointing dog it seems like shooting at box cars and the birds are hard to miss.

You understand, though, if you are walking with your mind far away and a pheasant jumps up from a little patch of grass directly behind you, it is okay to miss your shot. By the time you gather your wits about you, then take time to decide if the bird is a take-only rooster, he may be out of your comfort shooting zone.

When I retrieved my triple I looked around for Babe and saw her standing solid about 40 yards away, and I thought she was pointing at another pheasant. Usually when someone would shoot and down a bird, she is likely to be the first one to retrieve it.

When I got close to her I saw that her ears were relaxed and she had a disinterested attitude, and just looked at me when I talked to her. She would not move, and when I got close to her I finally noticed she was in a "sticker patch" and all four feet had several spines embedded in the pads.

I picked her up and carried her out of the patch, and she was very compliant as I laid her down and removed all of the stickers. Then she was back in the game again and was off at a slow trot with her nose almost on the ground, seeking birds.

The same morning we four were walking through a field in a line with the dogs in front of us, getting an occasional point, but as usual the pheasants were running ahead, and we were not very successful. I was on the outside of the line, and I saw a pheasant flush about 100 yards ahead. I pulled my gun up to my shoulder and shouted loud enough for my companions to hear, "Bang!" At such time, everyone looked to see what I was shouting about. What they did not know was that as soon as I shouted, the pheasant flew into a wire and fell dead way out of gun range. Four birds — and only three shots. Not a bad start for opening day. The only bad thing was my companions had to listen to me tell them this again and again all the way home

We hunted very long and hard, and after a couple of days everyone had bagged their limit, the dogs were worn out, and we were all very tired. We just drove around the country for another day or so looking at the successful farm lands.

We were told the farmers were mostly of German descent, and the older farm houses were extremely neat and all looked like they had a fresh coat of paint, as did all the barns. The lawns and trees around the houses were all picture-perfect.

The farm machinery was lined up in military fashion and also looked freshly painted, and were a contrast to the great wheat fields that had been harvested and re-sown with winter wheat.

This is the real Kansas that most people never see when rushing to Colorado on the super highways.

So we went back to the house where we stayed, picked up the frozen birds from the freezer, loaded all our gear and the dogs in the car, and we ended another successful hunt.

We began a long ride home, alternately sleeping and taking turns driving. This time we heard no complaints about the lingering smell we had started our hunt with.

Reflection

I have been startled many times when hunting or fishing. The jumping of an unseen pheasant practically under your feet is probably one of the most exciting. A quail under the same circumstances is exciting too. I have fished a lot in farm ponds after dark where black bass are waiting for you and have decided that the black top-water, noisy bait is just for them, and they decide to grab the lure right at your feet with a large, noisy splash. Keeping in mind that poisonous snakes are abundant in the area, and being cold blooded and probably not out at night, you might step on one waking both the snake and you up in a hurry.

It's exciting too if you are dozing in a duck blind and a bunch of ducks decide to visit you with a combined splash. And it's particularly exciting if you cannot put your hand on your gun while you are peeking through the willows on the front of the blind at the ducks.

The ultimate incident happened to me while having a nap on a sunny, no ducks flying afternoon, when a 12-point whitetail buck decides to swim across the river, walk across the sand bar in front of the blind, plunge into the 4 foot deep water among our decoys with an extremely loud noise, swim across our slough, then look down his nose at we invaders in his domain, and walk slowly into the willows behind us.

I am sure every hunter or fisherman has happenings that he remembers, whether it is a young son who has caught an 8 inch trout in an indoor pond at an outdoor show, or tangling with a giant Lake Trout in one of Canada's great northern fly-in lakes.

These memories all are worth keeping. Write them down. They all count. Someday.

Mark

Mark was a dog. My dog. His formal registered AKC name was "Mark of Kickapoo Bar" No. 25816. He was a Brittany spaniel and colored white and orange. He was of royal blood. His ancestors came from overseas. His father's name was "Pierrot De Mirabeau" AKC No. 32295.

Pierrot did break tradition, however, and chose a commoner name, "High Prairie Mamie" AKC No. 58382, to be the bearer of his family.

Mark's breeder was Mr. Charles F. Greever. Charles was a longtime executive of the famous old Missouri Bridge and Iron Company and a noted breeder of a long line of very large Brittany spaniel dogs.

I knew Mr. Greever only slightly, and we had a mutual friend, Mr. Rip Brown, who worked at the same place that I was employed. Mr. Greever could have sold the pups in this litter for top dollar, but he chose to give the pups to people who were dedicated sportsmen and would appreciate the dogs, and who would vigorously use them for what they were born for, to be hunted in the field instead of being someone's lapdog.

I picked up the little bundle of white, cuddly, furry puppy, but how could you not make a lapdog of him. Everyone who saw him had to pick him up, and he returned as much love as the person who held him loved him, always with a quick lick on the face if he got close enough.

Mark was born in early November, and I took him with me wherever I went most of the time. He had grown rapidly, and the following spring when he ran he was already showing the distinctly "rocking chair gait" that Brittany's have when they are running.

I introduced him to the Missouri River. He showed no fear and seemed to be born for the water. He was soon playing "fetch the stick" in the water, and in later years we had him in the duck blind as long as the water was not cold. When we sent him after a crippled duck, he would swim a long ways before he caught the duck or just finally gave up and came trotting up the river bank to the blind if he could not catch it.

Later in the summer when he was still a puppy it was a lot of fun watching him discover all the new smells in the prairie grass or woods. It was great seeing a quail flush from near to his nose that startled him momentarily, then see him try to run to catch the quail, and then come back to where the quail had set to get another nose full of quail smell and to see just what that was all about.

Mr. Greever told me one time that his old dogs were so automatic in their hunting that it was first, point, then hold position when the quail was flushed, then at command it was retrieve the downed bird and sit and hold the bird at the bosses feet until it was taken from them.

But when you have a young dog, you can never tell what it's going to do. Some will not point right away, and when they do point, they get nervous and flush the quail accidentally.

Sometimes they will not hold the point steady for long, and then they'll edge one hesitant step at a time and flush the quail. Sometimes they can't resist chasing after a rabbit and yelp as they run. And sometimes they will not respond to directions by voice, arm signals, or sometimes even a police-type whistle which is used if you are hunting in wide open fields.

I remember Mark's first point. It was the first day of quail season, and we were walking down a little-used road at the side of a field, and he pointed at a small clump of grass only about 15 feet from me.

He held the point solid, and when I could not see anything there, and Mark would not break the point, I grabbed him by his 4 inch tail, picked his rear end up, swung it 90 degrees, and set him down.

As I did this, a quail that was completely hidden with its camouflaged feathers right under Mark's nose, flushed away, flying only a couple feet above the ground and straight away from me.

I thought to myself that after all the work we put into hunting before the season opened, this is one shot I had better take my time with, and make sure I downed the bird. Which I did, but even though Mark was very interested in the quail he did not retrieve it, and he stayed with the quail until I got there to him.

I felt so proud of him and knew this point was to be the first of many, and he finally knew what all the training was about and what he was trained to do.

He joined me hunting in most of the state. We hunted quail all over eastern Kansas. We hunted quail in the Flint Hills of southeastern Kansas where he wore leather boots to protect his feet from the sharp, loose flint stones. We hunted pheasants in far western Kansas and the central Kansas prairies for Prairie Chickens. We hunted ducks and geese on the Missouri River.

In Nebraska, we hunted ducks on the Platte River near Grand Island and grouse in the north-central part of the state with good friend Bob Swiderski who had taken a new job and left Leavenworth before I did.

Every September we started off our hunting season shooting Mourning Doves as they returned from the grain fields across the Missouri River. We were on the Kansas side on a bluff some 100 feet above the river, and it made for very challenging shooting. Mark did not have a very soft mouth, and when he picked up a Dove he always had a mouth full of small feather which he did not like.

We hunted in all type of weather. One year when we had an early winter we were hunting quail, and we came to a pond that was frozen over. I am sure that was Mark's first exposure to ice. He ran across the pond and fell through the ice about 10 feet from the opposite bank. He finally managed to pull himself out of the water before I could get around the pond to help, and he lay on the ground and could not stand. His back legs and body were frozen.

By the time I got to him he was standing though, and back into his "hell bent for leather" mode and hunting again. Apparently he had enough body heat to melt the ice. A quick wipe down with a cloth and we were hunting again.

He saved me miles of walking when we were hunting ditches between harvested corn or wheat fields. He knew there were no birds in the fields and would move to the ditches seeking birds, and if none were there he would come back and we would move on to the next field.

Mark had no problem with barbed wire fences. He insisted on jumping over the top strand, until one day he did not clear the top wire and caught the inside of one of his back legs on a barb and was hanging by one leg. He made his situation clear to all, and when I rushed and freed him he was off and running to the next potential game bird habitat. After that he would travel up and down a fence row looking for an easy passage, and he jumped the top strand of the fence as a last resort.

It has always been my belief that dogs revert to their wild ancestral background with little or no warning. When I read where someone has been attacked by a single dog or multiple dogs, and seriously wounded or killed, it reconfirms my belief. Mark was no different.

One day when we were hunting on private land with the farmer's permission, Mark came upon a young hog that had strayed from its penned location and immediately attacked it. When I got to him he had the hog on the ground and was biting it in the stomach, just in front of the back leg. The hog was squealing very loud as I pulled Mark away and continued walking up the road.

The hog regained his feet, seemingly more frightened than hurt, and continued eating spilt corn on the ground. When we had gone about 75 yards away the hog made a noise, and Mark was after him again, and I had to go back and get Mark loose again. That was the last time I ever put him in a position to be with live hogs.

One day when I was at work, a salesman stopped in to visit and said he called on a man in Kansas City who had a bird dog he wanted to give away, and if I was interested, give him a call. And I did.

The man said the dog was a registered female English Pointer and she had gotten out of her pen and was now ready to have pups of mixed-breed. But he did not want to be bothered with taking care of her and her new family. I told him I would be down the next day, and he said he would bring her to his office for an easy pick up.

When I got to his office in Kansas City, I was not only greeted by a beautiful liver-and-white pointer, but also a box of new-born puppies. Now, instead of being a one dog family, I was the proud owner of two adults and six juvenile hunting dogs.

Nancy's Babe made an inauspicious introduction to my human family. When one of my sisters could not resist picking up one of the cute new puppies, she was given a nip on one of her fingers. But, being a mother herself, she understood about a mother protecting her little ones, and Babe became one of her favorites in a short time.

They got lots of loving care from my sister's four year old daughter and her eight year old nephew. We had misgivings, but soon found a home for the pups. They resembled their mother, and my hunting friends were anxious to take the little dogs. I have a picture of one of Babe's pups about six months old, holding a point on a tame quail. They were both on a picnic table in his back yard.

As long as I am writing about tame quail, I will always remember the most quail I have ever seen at one time. One of my hunting companions said he had some quail to show me, and since I was always ready for something like that, he led me to what I took for an abandoned hatchery building far from his house, and we went in very cautiously.

The second floor was a large room, and inside was a very noisy covey of 2,500 quail. They had bought the quail from someone who intended to market them to restaurants. My friend made a very low whistle with his mouth, and it was instant and complete silence. All the birds froze in one position and remained that way until they were sure they were safe, and then they were soon back to the noise we heard when we first came into the building. I was not living in Kansas then, and I never knew what happened to all the quail.

Mark had become used to being in the house in the winter if the weather was bad. But now that I had two dogs, and did not want them to be inside dogs in the winter. It was time for a dog house.

This was to be state-of-the-art dog house. It would be extremely austere, totally functional, with a removable center partition and roof. The building was 4 feet wide and 8 feet long. It had two doors on the front and a heavy cloth covering the door's opening. One side was for Mark, and one was for Babe. There would be blankets on the floor of the house and room for 2 or 3 inches of straw during the winter. Big mistake!

There was a time of very severe weather between Christmas and New Year's with the temperature hovering around 10 degrees, and I bought a bale of straw for the dog house floor. With that much straw it would enable me to freshen up the house with new straw occasionally.

I decided that perhaps the straw would not be enough to keep the dogs warm, so I bought a length of plumber's heating tape that was used to thaw out frozen household plumbing. I ran an electric wire to the house and folded the tape to cover both sides of the house.

I kept this tape turned on only at night, and it seemed to work very well. But since this time of the year is very busy, the tape was left turned on the night before and all day before New Year's Eve.

When I looked out to check the dogs the first thing New Year's Day, Mark was setting on the back stoop and Babe was out checking the neighborhood, and the state-of-the-art dog house had burned to the ground!

Not only did the dog house burn, but an ornamental fir tree was burned to about 8 feet above the ground. It should have burned totally, and was a wonder that it did not. I am convinced that with the additional heat and the dogs moving, the fire was started by static electricity.

The following occurred before the dog house fire. Now that I was the proud owner of two dogs, one young male and one experienced female, I realized I had certain obligations to fulfill, and when Babe came into season I took her to a boarding veterinary for a thirty-five day stay. This is longer than the normal thirty day time, and the veterinarian told me it was safe to let her loose with my male dog. Another big mistake.

I went to check on them later in the day, and what I saw was the dog house violently shaking. The loose partition was rattling, the roof was rising up and down, and I was not sure the whole thing would not collapse on the two dogs. It reminded me of one of the cartoons you used to see at the movies. I was back in the dog family way again.

Babe had her pups: half-English Pointer and half-Brittany Spaniel. The pups were odd-looking, with the Pointer's body and some of the curly hair from the Brittany showing up in different places. The exception was one beautiful, large male with all of the Pointer looks. He was dark liver-and-white like his mother, and the only thing that he got from his father was a little bit of bushy hair at the end of his tail. I gave him to one of my best friends, and I am not sure if he ever got to be hunted.

I thought that with Mark's lineage I could continue the strain of large Brittany's that Charley Greever had perfected, and when first someone came to me seeking Mark to breed to his female Brittany, I was anxious to comply. However, the female was very dominating, and there were no results.

The second time we had him bred was a success, and I had the pick of the litter. I chose a little male that was the exact duplicate of his father. The dynasty had started.

I had the ideal home for the new puppy. I gave him to my brother who I was sure would let me continue the lineage. No such luck. The puppy delighted in playing tug-o-war with my sister-in-law's washing that was drying on the clothesline, and he was given away to persons far away in southern Missouri without my knowledge. I never saw or heard of him again. Goodbye, dynasty.

In all of my hunting with my Brittany and Pointer dogs, they had to be transported in the trunk of my car. I drilled a 2 inch hole in one side of the trunk next to the rear window, but to one side. I brought a sliding tube that could be rotated to allow plenty of fresh air for the dogs and inserted it in the trunk hole.

I let the Brittany ride with me when we are not hunting, and I had him under my control. If you have been around a wet dog very much, I am sure you have experienced a strong dislike for their distinctive odor. But more than that, sometimes a dog seemed like it was forced to roll on its back on a diseased, smelly animal. They then carry the odor with them for some time.

At that time, I was driving a very large Buick sedan, and it was a great car, but it had a heavy trunk lid that was very hard to close.

One day we were in the field for a very long, hard hunt with a large amount of walking. After we decided to quit for the day, I was really tired, as were the dogs, and we had a long walk back to the car through a corn stubble field.

When we got back I put my gun in its case, took off my coat with the pheasants inside (my pointer loved to eat fresh game birds), watered the dogs, gave them a bit to eat, and they were very ready to get in the car and go home.

They were both sitting in the car waiting for the lid to close. I told them to "duck your head," which they did not do, and when I tried to close the trunk, the latch would not catch.

When I raised the trunk they raised their heads, and I tried to latch the lid, time and time again with no luck. The dogs seemed to wonder what I was doing, and the more I tried, the more upset I got. As a result, I repeated "duck your head" for the last time and slammed the trunk as hard as I could. I did not want to hurt the dogs, but my patience was at an end, and we drove home. The dogs showed no sign of damage and were anxious to get out of the trunk and to the food they had in the kennel.

There was a hold-over from this hunt. If I happened to catch one of the dogs sitting looking at me, all I had to do was raise my right hand and say "duck your head!" This brought an immediate response. The dog would collapse on the floor, looking up at me, waiting for the trunk to slam. Then when I spoke to him he felt released and bounced around, glad to be back in my good graces again.

So that was Mark of Kickapoo Bar. I changed jobs and moved to Chicago, and did not hunt for several years. Mark lived with my parents, and with only an occasional walk with my father to see if the Missouri River was still running, he did not get into the field again. This makes it difficult and very sad for me to write his story.

George's Diary

This chapter was not originally intended for this edition since the original concept was to be outdoor adventures, primarily hunting and fishing. I decided though that being deeply involved in wartime 1943, this would be an acceptable addition. And a mention later on of hand carved decoys and being homesick, plus the flight of migrating ducks, earns the chapter's right to be included.

My older brother, George Cord, was a volunteer seaman who early in World War II went through all the necessary things demanded by the Naval Great Lakes Training Center. It was located just north of Chicago, Illinois. No doubt through the ultimate wisdom of some Chief Petty Officer—who was impressed with George's wing shooting—George was delegated for gunnery school and was assigned as an armed guard on a Liberty Ship which was sailing from the East Coast to the European Theater of War. George spent most of his time shuttling men and material from North Africa to Italy.

He made several voyages, some as far as India and Burma. George kept a diary of each of these trips, and all but two diaries have been lost or confiscated by naval authorities. There was a lot of family interest in these writings, and each generation has been impressed and decided they were worth preserving. In each instance the interest had waned, but now is rising again.

The writings were written by pencil on onionskin paper, and they have withstood the hazards of time and the shuffling between potential family recorders amazingly well. I intend to try again to give a Kansas man's version of his little war.

Even though I know he felt quite at home on water, for a person whose largest exposure to any water other than the Missouri River, farm ponds, and the larger fishing lakes in Minnesota, it had to be quite a challenge to be pulling night watch on the bow of a small ship moving almost vertically up and down during hurricane type waves that were often taller than the ship itself.

Life at sea during war is a time of amazing contrasts. Days and weeks were spent sailing in the boiling sun with nothing to do except keep one's weapons functional, stand watch, read and write letters home. Then being awakened by the roaring of depth charges at night when the navy had discovered an enemy submarine traveling near or among the ships of the convoy.

The Liberty Ship my brother was assigned to was named the *U.S.S. Lincoln Steffens*. It was launched January 28, 1942 and was one of the first of that class of ship that used welding construction in its hull instead of the old, tried-and-true rivet construction. At this time welding was comparatively new, and not much information was available about welding together steel plates of different tensile strength. The ships developed long cracks along the hull, and the exposure to extreme cold while crossing the North Atlantic exacerbated this condition. The *Lincoln Steffens* was one of 2,751 Liberty Ships built, and they had a design life of only five years. Consequently only two remain afloat today.

There is no way I could improve on what is written in the logs, and I intend to quote them as written by George. I will make note when giving excerpts, but primarily I will give the actions taking place in a trip from North Africa to Naples, Italy.

This particular log took place between September 5, 1943 and February 15, 1944. George and his shipmates sailed from Norfolk, Virginia, to Oran, Algeria, North Africa. The voyage took a total of twenty days, and they were but one ship in a large convoy. The following was written while moored at Augusta, Sicily, November 16, 1943, after a sail from North Africa.

"Boy, this has been a long and nerve-racking five days. I did not have time to write. At 6:15 in the evening of November 11, five hours out of Oran, all hell broke loose. It was just getting dark when torpedo planes and high and low level bombers attacked us.

It was quite a mess for about 40 minutes: Ships getting hit and exploding or on fire all around us. The air was full of exploding shells and tracer bullets.

We dropped back out of the convoy because the water was covered with fire from a tanker filled with airplane gasoline that had caught on fire and blown up. That was a beautiful but horrible sight.

When we dropped back the planes must have thought we were hit because they ganged up on our ship. Man it was plenty hot for a few minutes. Our gun crew got official credit for knocking down two enemy planes. It was get them or they (would) get us."

Author's note: At that time, George must have had some remorse as he did not mention that when the planes first came after them, he was the first man of the gun crew to reach the guns. He activated the anti-aircraft gun, and since a plane was heading right into his line of fire, he single-handedly downed one plane. He got official credit and was awarded the Bronze Star Medal.

"In that short time I got about ten years older. Sometime during that raid something hit me on my tin hat and the hat was on my head. That was getting mighty close. I didn't even know it until the show was over. I guess it was a machine gun bullet."

Author's note: This next paragraph makes this story acceptable for a book primarily about hunting and fishing. George was an avid duck hunter and one who took pride in his hunting ability and his handmade duck decoys. These entries take place after an air raid while moored at a dock in Naples. Typical nautical expression: "No place to run, no place to hide." The Germans were bombing the city as well as all the ships in the harbor, and his only haven was below deck on his ship.

"Sometime during the excitement my box of decoys I made disappeared. I never missed them until I got to Naples. When I went to look for them all I had was a lot of splinters. They were sitting back on the stern in a box I had. There were seventeen all finished. Somehow a shell or something hit them. There will never be a way of telling how close it was. You could have heard me cussing all the way back home."

Author's note: The following occurred on another trip to Naples from North Africa.

"I went to bed with all my clothes and shoes on and my tin hat and life jacket where I could grab them and run. I sure thought they had us again Saturday night, the 13th of November.

High level bombers came over again dropping flares and we were under the only big cloud in the sky. I guess they didn't see us. Boy, talk about an awful feeling when those flares came down through the clouds that would turn your blood to ice water. I saw a big bunch of ducks go over this afternoon. They sure looked good to me."

Author's note: After all he had been through with the guns, all the big storms with gigantic waves that made the ship seem to be going up and down almost vertically, and the noise and the blazing heat coming on a southern route to the United States, Mother Nature had one more little thing planned to teach him some humility. He was standing watch on the bow of the ship during a storm just a few days outside their Brooklyn Naval Yard port.

"February 12, 1944 Saturday

It is really cold and a wild night tonight, with rain, sleet and snow. The wind is blowing a gale. The sea is wild and rough. It's a kind of a night that makes you wonder why you didn't stay on land. One good thing, there will be only 3 or 4 days of it at the most. It won't be too soon for me.

February 13, 1944 Sunday

This was a day to write home about. It has done everything but for the sun to shine. It rained and snowed all day long. Nearly got washed overboard this morning. We slipped an extra big wave over the bow this morning. I went all the way to the bridge. I never saw so much water all at once in so short a time. I thought I would freeze before I could get someone to relieve me so I could get some dry clothes on. Then the ensign moved the bow watch to bridge; some fun and that water sure was cold. Should be in New York sometime Tuesday the 14th."

So that's the story of some of George's naval life. He came through his total time unscratched, except the time the bullet creased his helmet. Late in the summer of 1945 he was on another assignment on a ship heading for Manila, Philippines, when the atomic bomb was dropped on Japan, and his boat turned around and sailed back to the West coast. He got back in time to join his older non-military friends for opening day of that fall's duck hunting

season on the river in a duck blind prepared and ready for him.
Home at last.

Author's note: Total time George observed ducks during hunting season in the fall of 1943: twenty minutes. One flight, north to south. First five-minutes: alarm for suspected enemy aircraft. Second five-minutes: flight verified as a mallard ducks flyover; all clear. Third five minutes: homesick inducer, ducks leaving. Fourth five minutes: back to possible enemy aircraft for ships on the southern horizon and then on to their winter quarters somewhere in Africa.

THE SECRETARY OF THE NAVY

WASHINGTON

The President of the United States takes pleasure in presenting the BRONZE STAR MEDAL to

GEORGE EDWARD CORD, GUNNER'S MATE THIRD CLASS
UNITED STATES NAVY

for service as set forth in the following

CITATION:

"For meritorious achievement as a Member of a Gun Crew serving in the Navy Armed Guard Unit on board the U.S.S. LINCOLN STEFFENS in action against enemy aircraft off the Coast of Algeria, November 11, 1943. Cool and courageous when his convoy was attacked from different sectors of the screen by hostile bombers and torpedo planes, CORD gallantly carried out his vital duties despite heavy crossfire from other ships of the convoy and the intensity of the attack, contributing materially to the heavy barrage of fire thrown up by our guns and the subsequent shooting down of one enemy plane and probable destruction of several others. By his steadfast devotion to duty, CORD was instrumental in enabling a valuable convoy to continue on its essential mission and upheld the highest traditions of the United States Naval Service."

For the President,

James Forrestal

Secretary of the Navy

George's Citation for the Bronze Star Medal

A SAILOR'S DREAMS

SOMETIMES WHEN THE EVENINGS ARE UNUSUALLY LONG AND QUIET, I LAY DREAMING OF PEOPLE, PLACES AND THINGS BACK HOME.

IT IS EASY TO DREAM THAT I'M ON SOME SMALL LONELY LAKE IN THE NORTH WOODS, WHERE THE WOODED SLOPS OF TALL PINE, REACH ALL THE WAY DOWN TO THE WATERS EDGE.

INSTEAD OF BEING TOSSED AROUND BY THE BIG WAVES OF THE ATLANTIC, WHILE ON BOARD SOME FREIGHTER, I'M RIDING MY CANOE ON WATERS THAT ARE STILL, CALM AND SMOOTH AS A MIRROR.

THERE IS NO LARGE ANTI-AIRCRAFT GUN MOUNTED ON HER BOW, NOTHING BUT A PADDLE. IN MY HANDS, INSTEAD OF A RIFLE OR A MACHINE GUN I CAN FEEL MY FAVORITE CASTING ROD.

HIGH OVER HEAD, A MEAR SPECK IN THE BLUE, WHEELING AND DIPPING AN EFFORTLESS WING, SAILS NOT A FIGHTER PLANE BUT A HAWK IN SEARCH OF EVENING MEAL.

TWO DUCKS COME SAILING IN ON BRACED WINGS, LOOKING ALL THE WORLD LIKE TWO DIVE BOMBERS, AND DROP INTO THE REEDS AT THE EDGE OF THE LAKE.

BUBBLES RISING TO THE SURFACE ARE NOT FROM A DEADLY TORPEDO BUT JUST A LAZY TURTLE SWIMMING ALONG. AND AN EVER WIDENING "V", CATCHING AND REFLECTING THE RAYS OF THE SETTING SUN IS NOT THE PERISCOPE OF A LURKING SUBMARINE, BUT A BUSY BEAVER'S HARD AT WORK.

A LOUD SPLASH BACK IN THE WEEDS IS NOT THE EXPLOSION OF A BOMB, BUT A FISH LEAPING AND BREAKING THE RESTFUL SOLITUDE OF THE QUIET WATERS.

THE SUN SETS AND THE COOL OF EVENING DECENDS. SOON THE WORLD IS STILL AND COVERED WITH DARKNESS. IT MUST BE NICE TO BE IN A WORLD SO PEACEFUL WITHOUT WAR, BUT I DON'T SEEM TO BE ABLE TO REMEMBER QUITE THAT FAR BACK.

S 1/C   GEORGE E. CORD   USNAVY

A wartime entry from George's diary.

55

Missouri Valley Steel

Missouri Valley Steel was a structural fabricating shop that was a spin-off of the old Missouri Valley Bridge and Iron Company based in Leavenworth, Kansas. They not only had a similar name, but they inherited a structural steel fabricating shop, a shipyard on the bank of the Missouri River, and a warehouse dating from the early 1920s or before. They also inherited a bunch of workers who had worked for the old Bridge and Iron Company.

Their old company was a nationally-known designer and builder of deep water bridge piers. One of their most famous bridge pier jobs occurred when a company trying to sink the piers on the famous Oakland Bay Bridge in California could not successfully sink them, and the Bridge and Iron Company was given the job to finish the piers. The old company had much more experience and completed the project in record time.

The old warehouse, if it was intact today, would be a very interesting museum of deep water bridge building. What I saw were the old round helmets with the round screw-on face masks hung as if they were ready to be worn on the job. Each helmet was attached to the full-body suits that were part of the "sand hog's" working clothes. The remainder of the building was filled with what was apparently diver support paraphernalia. There was an abundance of rubber hoses and air compressors. There was also many hand earth moving tools that were dusty from long use, but I could see no rust on them.

The second floor of the building was being used as a template shop for barge and tug boat shell layout. Probably the same type of work was done there in template construction by the old Bridge and Iron Company.

The shipyard was located on south Second Street in a low area right on the river bank, making it easy to launch the just-made river barges and tug boats. A problem occurred occasionally when the June rise of the river flooded the shipyard and halted all construction until the flood subsided.

The shipyard was very active in late World War II in the building of U. S. Navy Landing Craft. Missouri Valley Steel contracted for and built fourteen 65-five-foot long passenger-cargo vessels for the U. S. Army. They followed up with a contract for twenty-eight 65-foot-long Harbor Tugs. This contract was finished in early 1953.

One of the hold-over workers at the Pennsylvania Street fabricating plant was a man named Toby who had worked on the same small machine for forty-five years. I think it was an anchor bolt forming machine.

Occasionally some of the older workers would get an opportunity to display some of their hidden but not forgotten talents. As late as the early-50s, welding was the accepted manner of attaching pieces of structural steel together for most jobs. That is, except for railroad bridges and certain large automobile highway bridges. Occasionally, a railroad bridge or a highway bridge was awarded, and all the structural steel angles and plates had to be riveted together. Apparently, the heavy vibration of the passing freight cars or heavy trucks put additional stress on welds, and the railroad or bridge designers were not ready to accept welding as their standard yet.

When the large Centennial Bridge was to be built to span the Missouri River at Leavenworth to replace the very old railway

bridge, then converted to automobile traffic at Fort Leavenworth, Missouri Valley Steel Company bid and was awarded the contract for the approach structures on both sides of the bridge.

The bridge approaches were to be plate girder design, and rivets were to be used in the fabrication. The two girders would be 5 feet high and approximately 500 feet long on each side extending from the arches out to the built-up roadway from the flat bottom land on the east in Missouri to the built-up roadway on the west in Kansas. This job was finished and erected on time, and is a tribute to the working men of Leavenworth.

When it came time to rivet the plates and angles together, several of the older men who grew up using rivets were ready to go. They still had the furnaces to heat the bolts with the round heads, the tongs to pick up the red hot bolts and toss them some 10 to 15 feet to where the rivets would be caught by a man holding an iron cup.

After the rivet was caught, the man with the cup would grab the rivet with another pair of tongs and place the hot bolt into a hole in the plates waiting to be riveted. Then a man with an air compressor tool would put it against the hot rivet, while another man on the opposite side of the rivet would hold a head-forming tool against the rivet while it was being hammered. The opposite head of the rivet would be hammered into a perfect half circle to match the opposite side. This made a very tight connection.

These men were very good at their work, and after a couple of dropped rivets, the only one having trouble was the young man bucking the back of the rivet who probably had never even seen a rivet until someone handed him the tool and said you are a riveter now.

During one of many trips through the shop, I got to know most of the older workers and knew the man catching the rivets. His name was Pauly, and he told me he used to catch the rivets without the iron cup using only the tongs. He said that was the only way he could keep up with the two men doing the riveting.

I jokingly told Pauley I had come down to see somebody catching thrown hot rivets in the air with tongs, not a tin cup, like he told me he used to do. Pauly was ready for the challenge. The rivets were small rods with a round head ¾ inches in diameter and about 2 to 3 inches long, and when the hot rivet was tossed to him he was catching eight out of ten with the tongs after he got his timing back.

The Missouri Valley Steel Shipyard was on the Missouri River where they built big river barges. Again, in the past, before they were using welding, the steel plates had to be riveted together. The barges were built in large sections with a lot of room to perform the riveting tasks, but when it came time to put the sections together, there had to be someone inside the big dark barges to buck the back of the rivets.

Kansas in the summer can be quite a bit hotter than one would like it to be, and working on the inside of a barge handling red hot rivets can be very unpleasant. It is not easy to keep your mind on your body temperature when the hammering of the rivets makes you think of being on the inside of some giant drum. It was definitely a job for a healthy young man, and it would be right up there with the TV show "Dirtiest Jobs."

The pride of Michigan bridges is the 5-mile-long giant Mackinaw Bridge tying the Upper and Lower Peninsulas together. A couple of the big barges used in the erection of the structural steel, or the piers, were fabricated at the Leavenworth shipyard. I repeatedly remind my companions, or anybody else within earshot during my travels in Michigan, of this great accomplishment.

There are still tow boats fabricated by the shipyard that are in use on United State's rivers. One tow boat in particular has an interesting story about when it was being delivered from Leavenworth to Memphis, Tennessee.

A national railroad needed a tow boat, where the most important criteria in tug design was maneuverability, to ferry railroad freight cars that were stacked on barges across the Mississippi River from Memphis to the freight yards in Arkansas.

Somewhere, one of the Missouri Valley officers had obtained two giant U. S. Navy surplus diesel generators, and after a long time they were about to find a home.

Missouri Valley had signed a contract to build the boat and started construction. The design of the boat was not the typical engine-driveshaft propeller construction. It was to be a diesel electric propulsion system. There were two large circular electric motors lying on their sides with a vertical shaft sticking below the boat into the water.

Each of these shafts was attached to a propeller that served to drive the boat with 360 degrees capability. The important thing about the two propellers was that they were able to operate independently which gave the boat great maneuverability.

The boat was built and underwent long testing on the Missouri River. On one of the shake-down cruises the boat had a minor fire which was extinguished. The main problem was telling the officer of the company about the fire when he was in the hospital with a heart problem that was finally corrected.

The boat was finally inspected and ready for delivery to Memphis. The boat was captained by the number-two man in the shipyard, Mr. Skip Higgins. He was the one who conducted most of the trial run testing on the river.

The boat started on the trip to Memphis via the Missouri River. It was 397 river miles to the Mississippi River, not far north of St. Louis,

Missouri. The auto trip to the Mississippi River from Leavenworth was some 255 miles, so you can see that the river does quite a bit of wandering through the state of Missouri.

Once the boat got into the Mississippi River they had to pass through the ship channel around the "Chain of Rocks" area near St. Louis and travel 413 miles to the city of Memphis, totaling 813 river miles.

To the best of my knowledge, the trip past the city of St. Charles was uneventful, but when they entered the Mississippi River there was an emergency SOS broadcast on the tug's radio. The call was from a tow boat captain with a string of barges that had lost his power, and he needed help in a hurry. The boat was floating down river, unable to make the entry into the ship channel around St. Louis, and was heading into the dangerous "Chain of Rocks" area in the center of the river.

Before the ship channel was built, boat travel had to cease in low water times, and there would be a string of boats both above and below the rocks waiting for the river to rise in order to safely pass the rocks.

The Missouri Valley boat's captain, Skip Higgins, talked to the floating barges captain, got his location, and said he was on his way.

Skip quickly found the tow in distress, and when he pulled up alongside and the captain saw the new boat he questioned Skip, "Do you think that boat can push all my barges?" Skip had a classic answer. "I don't know. I've never tried pushing anything with the boat as yet." But when the two boats were joined together, the Missouri Valley boat pushed the entire loaded barges and dragged the floating captain and his boat to safety.

Missouri Valley Steel was active in furnishing some structural steel during the cold war in the 1950s that went into the various Atlas Missile sites located around Wichita and Salina, Kansas, and Lincoln, Nebraska.

Some of the material was as simple as floor grating for platforms and stairways to the bottom of the silos. These grates were sometimes as small as 24" x 36" and were delivered to the site in

Missouri Valley Steel Sends
First of Boats Down the Ways

summer. They weren't put into place until in winter, and they were hard to find when covered up with snow. The general contractor would assume they had not been shipped, and it was our job to dig through the snow to find the missing pieces.

The opposite extreme in size and weight was the giant blast door that was against the silo wall and was meant to protect those inside from the extreme pressure during a missile firing. The floor grating weighed as little as 40 pounds each, and the 4' x 8' x 5" thick doors could weigh over 6,000 pounds. If I recall correctly, the latching mechanism was reminiscent of a typical barn door system and surely would be a contrast to the thick door.

I visited the silos a few times, and the only time I was in danger of being hurt was when I drove into a vacant parking lot near one of them around Wichita. I parked one space over from a small, white tanker truck with a bit of white smoke seeping from its rear.

I was out of my car with my briefcase heading into the building when two men dressed in white protective clothing came out of the building and questioned me about my visit. They told me to get back in the car, and whatever I did I was not to touch the key to the car.

They pushed my car far back from the building and told me that it was safe to continue my business inside. What I did not realize was that the tanker truck was loaded with liquid oxygen, and if a spark from starting an automobile was generated, the whole tank could explode. Needless to say, I am always aware in my highway travel now to avoid a truck with a printed Liquid Oxygen decal on it.

There are two structures in Leavenworth that are a tribute to the working people at Missouri Valley Steel that go unrecognized and are in use by hundreds or thousands of people every day, and are literally hidden from view. They are the steel plate girders I mentioned earlier that were fabricated locally to hold up the roadways that lead to the graceful arches of the Centennial Bridge linking Missouri and Kansas over the Missouri River.

These structures are an integral part of the bridge, and the

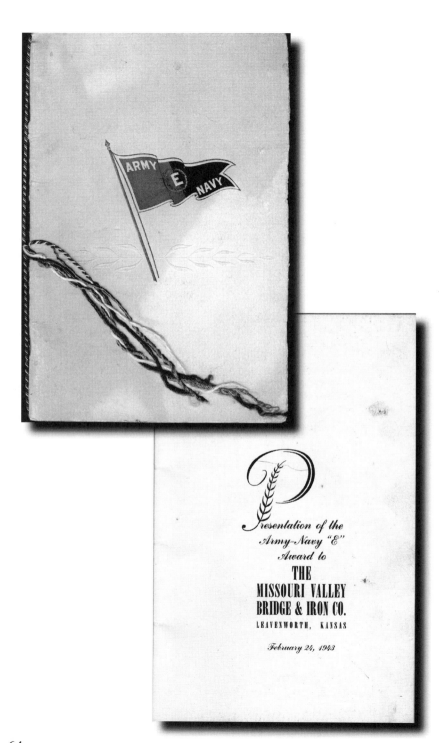

The Significance of the Army-Navy "E"

The Army-Navy production award is a salute from our fighting forces to the soldiers of industry. The flag which symbolizes this award has a rich tradition in the history of our armed forces. In 1906 the Navy instituted in the Fleet an award for Excellence which has been known ever since as the Navy "E". First awarded for excellence in gunnery, this was later extended to include outstanding performance in Engineering and Communications.

From the demand for increased production brought on by the war, the Award was extended to embrace both Army and Navy industrial activities.

An honor not easily won nor lightly bestowed the Army-Navy "E" carries great patriotic challenge and entails a pledge of service from us all. To fly this pennant with honor, our standards must be continued and even bettered.

girders on the west side of the bridge reach from the arches some 500 feet just past Second Street. The structure on the east side of the arches is identically designed and is about as long as the west side.

I happened to arrive in Leavenworth the day before the fiftieth year anniversary celebration of the bridge's opening and was surprised no one from the old Missouri Valley Steel company was to be involved. But by then the company had had a giant fire that destroyed the fabricating shop and the old warehouse, and I guess no one was contacted.

There were local and state dignitaries on hand, as was my good friend, Mr. Robert Seute, who was the last toll collector. No one there apparently knew about the locally fabricated approaches to the bridge, so I wrote a brief history and passed it along, but it did not get in the newspaper that week.

So that's the obvious contrast. The shipyard stands vacant, and all the boats, barges, and tugs for the U. S. Army are gone, and no trace of them exists.

The Centennial Bridge approaches will stand for a long time in Leavenworth. Local people will use the bridge hundreds of times a day, or maybe thousands, and only a few will see the girders if they happen to visit the park or boat ramp below the bridge.

I have always delighted in old bridges, and if I have an hour to spend waiting for someone, I can pass the time quickly if I have a pencil and paper and do simple bridge truss stress designs.

If I am traveling in rural eastern Kansas or western Missouri, I will go a long distance out of my way to see an old abandoned steel bridge and hope to find a dated bronze plaque of the Missouri Valley Bridge and Iron Company still in place after sixty or more years. The plaques have become a collector's item for historians. It is rare now to find the plaques at eye level, and the most common place to find them is on the cross member at the top of the bridge entry. I do have a bridge plaque, but it was never used and was given to me by one of the officers of the old bridge company.

The last old, small Missouri Valley Bridge and Iron Company bridge closest to Leavenworth is at Beverly, Missouri, on the old river route to Weston. It was condemned and not safe for automobile traffic now, but I have driven over it in the past and do not know if it is still standing.

What I have written is a very short history of Missouri Valley Steel and the things that I was associated with. I've done no justice to the Missouri Valley Bridge and Iron Company. There is a vast amount of knowledge available in the *Leavenworth Times* files at the local library, and it would be a major effort to do it justice.

Fall Hunting

Before I left Leavenworth, Kansas, and took a job in Chicago—a move that was unheard of among my many friends because no one ever moved to Chicago—I thought I had the world by the tail. When I got out of the Army, I was welcomed back by my old employer and was eager to get back on my old drawing board in the engineering department of Missouri Valley Steel, a local structural steel fabricator. I was out of the Army on a Thursday and back to work on the following Monday.

My desk faced north, right next to a large window, to get the best daylight to shine on my drawing board. I was not married then, and I took my yearly vacation only in the fall during the bird hunting season.

North lighting was a benefit I learned as a youth working for my sister while trying to select the five or six different shades of the tobacco leaves we were stripping from the stalks and tying into hands for sale at the tobacco warehouse in Weston, Missouri. Back then they had the old-fashioned sales with the auctioneer, several tobacco company buyers, and growers following down between the fresh tied hands in big round baskets. The farmer's big tobacco barns always had a stripping room with a series of windows facing north.

That was not the only reason why I liked my northern exposure. In the fall during the migratory waterfowl hunting season I could not help but look out the window, and if there was any indication that a flight was in progress, I was free to head for our cabin about thirty minutes away on the Kansas side of the Missouri River at Kickapoo, Kansas. And if our decoys were still in place, I could be hunting in about an hour and a half.

We hunted every weekend, and if a lot of ducks were around, my hunting partner, Bob Swiderski, and I would be in the blind long before daylight during the week to catch the early morning activity, and be back at work by nine o'clock. If I had a hot project on my drawing board, I would catch up missed time at night.

When I got back to work, my working companions who came in at eight o'clock would have just finished re-hashing previous night's activities like bowling scores, football scores, missed putts, pilot lessons, etc. And maybe have the first coke of the day, enhanced by the smoky taste that first cigar of the day always gives. Now we could all start working together by nine o'clock.

As you can tell, I had understanding and forgiving bosses. It was allowed that if a huge migratory flight was underway I was free to be absent until the flight was over, and if night work was required, I was always available.

The following is an attempt to describe the type of bird hunting that was available in Kansas at that time.

We started preparing for the duck and goose hunting on the river bank by staking out a place that would permit adequate water for decoy placement, was not too deep, with the current moving very slowly or not at all, and ideally against a bank where a dug-in blind could be made.

We cut enough willow saplings to push into the mud along the bank indicating we would be there hunting when the season was open. This usually occurred about the first week of August, and if the river rose, or the current shifted and the markers washed away, we had to stake out a place again.

August is a time when one should be working with his bird dogs if he intends to hunt them hard during the coming quail and pheasant hunting season. Bird dogs can be worked on quail at this time of year, but harming them is not allowed. It is fun to see a very small quail display his survival instincts. They seem to be about as big as a silver dollar, 1890 vintage, and take off from under your pointing bird dog's nose with a little whirr and a speed superman would be proud to admire.

The migrating Mourning Dove hunting season opened September 1st and lasted until October 1st. If an early cold-weather front came through the doves could be gone south as early as the first week of the season. These fast flying birds present a challenging target because of their erratic flight patterns, especially if a brisk wind is blowing.

The doves are indeed the poor man's experience of wild bird hunting. No fancy hunting clothes or boots required, no bird dog to be kept all year long for just a few hunts, no travel required, and the doves are everywhere. A lot of hunts start by picking up the shotgun with a pocket full of shells, and you are in business. Plus the doves are very good to eat.

I have been trying for years, searching in every bird book that I could get my hands on, to identify a local bird from my early youth, to no avail. The bird was called the "Rain Crow," and I have finally found it.

Earlier this past summer I was sitting in my sister's kitchen one gloomy, early morning where everything was very quiet and almost dark outside. It was one of those times where one would say "it looks like it could rain any minute."

Out of a clear blue sky, hardly fitting the day, she said "Rain Crow." I asked her what she said, and she repeated the two words. I was listening to the bird too, and what she heard was the mournful voice of a Dove. I had found the elusive "Rain Crow."

In this type of weather Doves have a call completely different from the usually soft, low call we associate with mating or when they are nesting. This mourning call is probably how the Dove got its name. If you have Doves in your neighborhood, listen, and you will know when you hear the mourning call and you'll never forget it.

The government-controlled migratory wildfowl hunting dates were established into hunting flyways. The Missouri River was the dividing line between the Mississippi and Central Flyways, and the opening and closing dates varied by at least one week. We had hunting licenses for both states that allowed us an extra week of hunting each year. The hunting dates usually ran from early October through November.

The scarcity of ducks made the bag limits only a very few ducks, and a lot of hunters decided not to pursue the sport until the daily limit was raised. We very seldom bagged a goose then, and now the Snow Goose population has exploded and a daily limit on the big birds is twenty a day in the fall, and no limit during spring migration.

The Bobwhite Quail season came along in November, but we did not hunt quail. We thought a good day on the river during a flight was worth a week's good quail hunting. That attitude changed when a friend gave me a Brittany spaniel puppy that I named "Mark of Kickapoo Bar" after our duck hunting area. Overnight I was a quail hunter.

The Ring-necked Pheasant season opened for a short time in early November, and that called for a 300-mile trip to northwest Kansas, and if conditions were right, a one day duck hunt in the Cheyenne Bottoms Wildlife area on our way west. Cheyenne Bottoms was a state-controlled flooded area in central Kansas with concrete blinds scattered about that were available during the hunting season on a regular early morning drawing for the best located blind.

The hunting season usually ended in early December and then in later years a goose season sometimes opened for a few days in January. We did not hunt then. All of our blinds were on the Missouri side of the river, and we left then intact after the waterfowl season ended. By early May when the river got to its original water level, we could see them from the Kansas side of the river and watch them gradually wash away, leaving the bank the way we found it in the previous August. The cycle was complete, and it was time now to think about wild mushrooms and fishing.

The U.S. Army Corps of Engineers controlled the rate of flow and the volume of water to be released from the four big dams on the Missouri River. Usually the flow was decreased during the last part of the duck hunting season, and the river depth would drop 2 to 4 feet or more.

This would mean sand bars would begin to be visible on the side of the river across from our cabin. The formation of the sand bar ideally gave us about 50 feet of decoy water between the sand bar and our duck blind dug into the far bank. This calm water was more attractive to decoying ducks.

When the temperature dropped below freezing for a few days, far up the river ice would form. The slowdown of the rate of flow of the water made for the formation of ice along the banks, and the ice would break away and create floes some 4 to 14 feet in diameter and 4 to 8 inches thick.

This meant if the ice had open areas large enough to let us maneuver our boats, we would do our best to get across the river to

our decoys. We would break up the ice in our sough in front of the blind, and since the ducks did not like to land in the river with all the ice, we had a natural place for passing ducks to land and rest.

To get to our blinds we had to cross the river in our small 14 or 16 foot flat-bottom boats, and the river can be treacherous in the winter. We did not hesitate to launch the boats if the river was partially filled with huge ice floes if there was enough distance between floes to maneuver the boat, but if the openings started to close we had to make haste to return to the Kansas side where our cabin was located. Sometimes we had to leave in a hurry and leave our decoys in the water, and hope they would be there when the ice quit running.

Our cabin was located about a quarter of a mile north of its present location. It seemed the Missouri River had a mind of its own and decided to change channels, and was very rapidly under-cutting the bank in the front of the cabin.

So we had no choice. We could gather and watch the cabin gradually sink into the rapidly flowing river, or take the cabin down and move the parts downstream, and re-erect the cabin away from the eroding river bank. The cabin was on the outside of a bend in the river, and it was very common in a flood stage for the current to shift to that side of the river.

I remember when I was a pre-teenager making a camp on the opposite side of the river and spending the night under a canvas lean-to while my father and a friend tended a dozen or so bank fishing lines every two hours. All night long we could hear loud splashes across the river as large pieces of bank, along with some huge trees, fell into the water.

Recently I found a handwritten account of a problem my grandfather had while working on the river. This is a copy someone had made of an article in the *Leavenworth Times*:

> "March 31, 1881. Startling, If True. It was reported that three raftsmen were struck by a falling bank and drowned.
>
> A report was current on the streets last night at 12 o'clock that three men who were bringing a raft of logs down the river were drowned yesterday afternoon near Kickapoo, Kansas. The names of only two of the men could be learned. One was George Amos Cord whose home is on Pawnee Street between Third and Fourth Street, and the other man was John Hines, who for some time had been boarding with Mr. Cord's Mother on Pawnee Street.
>
> The particulars as learned are so meager as to cause a doubt about the affair, but the report is that three men were managing a raft, keeping it near the Kansas shore, and that at a point near Kickapoo, a huge bank of earth fell over on top of the raft, completely covering the men and smothering them so they could not extract themselves.
>
> Mr. Smith, who lives in north Leavenworth, started for Kickapoo last night to learn further particulars. The shore at Kickapoo has been falling in rapidly at late, and it would not be strange if the report is true."

It was this same area that the *Leavenworth Times* reported

in their "One Hundred Years Ago" column of March 1981 that my grandfather, along with another man, while working on a raft of logs, was swept overboard and was drowned. Since my father was born in the fall of 1882, I couldn't wait to see what the paper would report next. The following day they reported there was a problem but both men had survived.

The cabin was rebuilt by five men: my brother, George, and the others were George Lowenheimer, Eugene Young, John Kirsh, and Joe Smith. I joined them in time when they decided their duck hunt and fishing cabin was going to be undercut and fall into the river. If they wanted to have a place to hunt out of the following fall, it was time to dismantle the cabin and rebuild in a safer place.

It was panic time, and working long after dark, the majority of the cabin was removed and trucked to the new site downstream, still on the Kansas side.

They all knew of the probability of flooding, and we still had the dreaded "June raise," which with heavy rain combined with snow runoff could put the river out of its banks, and the water would stretch from bluff to bluff.

That necessitated finding a huge wooden piling floating in the river or aground on a sand bar. These pilings were about 12 inches in diameter and about 30 feet long, and were driven in long rows against an eroding bank to try to control the location of the center of the current. Occasionally, one piling would get away from the pile driver and float in the river. This piling is what we needed to place vertically under the cabin's floor to keep it above a flooding river. The tough part was floating them to the cabin site behind a motor boat, and then sawing them into about 6 foot lengths. Sawing was by a huge gang saw handled by two men.

The pilings were spaced at about 5 foot centers through the soon-to-be cabin and stood about 3 feet above the ground. These pilings lasted for the life of the building, and whenever the water got out of its banks it left a layer of mud and sand that solidified the foundation even more.

The cabin was about 16' x 24' and had a front screened-in porch with a sloping roof facing east, and when it was built it had a perfect view of the river, nestled in a grove of big trees.

    The finished cabin only had a small amount of flood water on the floor until the 1993 flood which was a five hundred year expectancy depth, and it covered the floor with a huge amount of mud. By this time the cabin had very little use, and it was later intentionally burned to the ground because what was once a heavily wooded setting was now all cleared, and a very successful farming operation was being run by the third-generation Schwartz family. Having an unattended vacant wooden building surrounded by very tall trees with the potential of fire from lightning strikes that could spread to a drying farm crop and a nearby maintenance building meant the building had to go.

    The building was still located in the big bend in the river, and the Corps of Engineers had built a long dyke out of pilings that ended at our front door. There was no more erosion or falling banks to worry about.

    But no matter what I write, it seems to lead back to duck hunting. We had a good hunting area. The daily limit went from twenty-five birds a day back in the early 1930s to two or three a day. Hunting geese and ducks for commercial use was not allowed. Using live calling decoys was also outlawed.

But what really made a difference in our hunting area was the building of a huge, coal fired power plant some half mile north of us on the Missouri side of the river. The plant has huge water cooling ponds that lured the migratory ducks who lit there instead of the river. Also there is a power line that spans the river, and since ducks will not fly under a cable like that or under a bridge, we no longer attracted ducks flying low and following the channel in the river. This all happened after the Corps of Engineers had done major reworking of the whole river from its mouth all the way through most of Montana.

The cabin was used all year long. In the spring, morel mushrooms were waiting to be picked. There was a fresh fish market in the front yard. Fish-fry parties were always on the front burner. Late summer was time to get ready for the fall hunting. Then there was the river. A cruise up the river on a hot summer's afternoon was what tied our whole cabin experience together.

It is easy to look back at all the good times we had, and only try to remember some of the hard times.

Some years when there was not enough water against the 6-foot bank to dig a blind into, we had to dig a pit blind in the sand bar. If a strong south wind would blow right up the river we would be faced with a strong sand storm in our faces, and when we stood up we got sandblasted, and there were no ducks flying.

It was cold. Late season hunting brought big flocks of large yellow-legged Mallard ducks from their Canadian nesting grounds, and we had to be there hunting. This usually meant there was probably going to be ice in the river, and there was a chance you could get trapped across the river from the cabin.

If the wind blew from the south against the river flow, it caused choppy little waves that created small icicles on the bills of our bouncing decoys that had to be removed, probably by walking. Having a boat in the decoys when a flight of ducks flew over them was not good.

The decoys were placed from a boat, and sometimes when knocking the ice off the decoys one would step in an unknown hole that would add a boot of freezing water to one's misery.

If a bagged duck was lying where there was a small amount of current and had to be retrieved with the boat and outboard motor, everyone would volunteer to be the retriever because a short walk to the boat would tend to loosen joints from sitting for a long time in the blind.

There was, however, another problem. Most of the time the outboard motor would not cooperate and fail to start on the first pull of the cord, or the second, or the fifteenth. At this time exterior coats would start to come off and all stiffness was forgotten, and probably be welcomed back.

Meanwhile, the downed duck is floating farther away. The other hunters in the blind would be yelling encouragement to the retriever, then rapidly change to warning as a flock of ducks seemed to be very interested in the decoys and were swinging to get a closer look, when they spotted the man in the boat, now fully sweated down and standing up pulling the outboard motor's starting cord. At this point the ducks would flare away and continue their way south to a warmer climate and less hostile environment.

After being in the blind before daylight, the hot coffee long gone, and twelve o'clock dinner consumed before 9:00 A.M., with no heat in the blind, poor boy of Thunderbird or Silver Satin wine long gone, it was time for the real miserable task.

The weather forecast predicted below freezing temperatures for the next ten days, and if the decoys were not picked up that day, all 127 of them, including geese, might be frozen in the ice until spring.

The procedure is this: Pick up individually by hand. Knock off ice formed on decoy's back and bill. Wrap 4-foot decoy string around duck's body. Wrap 6-inch lead weight strip around ducks neck. Place decoy in gunny sack. (Rubber backed gloves kept hands dry, to a point, but still your hands got very cold.)

Usually some 100 decoys would require two boat loads, so one boat would cross the river, unload the sacks of decoys, and cross back over the river for the rest.

Once the decoys were carried back to the cabin, the heavy motor must be carried away and the boat man-handled up the river

bank and chained to a heavy log for safe keeping. And then, since the fire in the stove had not been tended all day, the cabin was no longer warm and friendly.

Now all the individual things must be gathered and loaded into the cars. There were guns, .50 caliber metal machine gun boxes full of non-used shotgun shells showing wear from loading and ejecting, long, cold thermos bottles, duck and goose calls, and hunting knives, etc.

Lastly, it's how to get back on the concrete road and safely home. We had to travel about a half mile of bottom land through the woods, up and over the railroad tracks, up the steep hill to the little town of Kickapoo, head south across the Plum Creek bridge, up another hill, then an easy trip to Highway 73.

Sounds simple, but. In the winter, the two hills that must be driven up are not friendly in rainy weather, and much worse if there was snow or ice on the roads. Often the only way to make the hills was the application of chains, or if no chains, an all-hands-but-driver effort pushing from the back made possible the ascension.

Next day we'd talk to everyone about "if the weather holds we may be able to make it next weekend."

Big Muddy Mud Cats

Most of the stories in this book are my own experiences. There are, however, some situations written that I did not get involved with, such as a hand-to-paw fight with a 350 pound black bear, even though six huge hounds were on my team. Until that is, I happened to touch one of the dogs without him knowing I was trying to help him. This qualifies me for the dummy of the year award and a permanent big dog bite scar.

Another thing I never expect to do is put my hand into the mouth of a huge catfish and try to drag him up through shallow water and a slippery, muddy river bank in the black of night. In the meantime, the fish is trying to separate your hand from your wrist, or at least trying to peel what skin you have left on both sides of your hand. Putting my hand into the mouth of a giant catfish, or as some hand fishermen do, put their arm up the elbow in the fishes mouth and out through the gills for a better capture hold, is something for me to avoid at all costs.

The following story is by my new friend, Rick Olsen. He has chosen to disregard the dangers of big cat fishing, and fishes almost only at night. A lot of his biggest catches happen in the few hours after midnight.

He is aware of the problems of fishing where you can only see the top of the water. He is aware of the presence of the huge Alligator Gar of the southern states. I am not sure they have been this far north, but I am pretty sure they are in the Mississippi River tributaries.

And what about global warming? If the temperature of the river water warmed a few degrees, and the big gars were found this far north, it would make all the skinny-dipping kids in the old swimming holes an exciting time. That would also require Rick to have at least a .45 caliber pistol as part of his tackle box.

Ordinarily, when I get a story from an outside source it requires a lot of arm twisting and pleading to get the actual events. This did not happen in the story of Rick's account of one midnight trip fishing for giant catfish. In this endeavor he has been outstanding. He has furnished me a great story of man against a

79

giant catfish one dark night while fishing recently with his wife and little girl on, and in, the Missouri River. He graciously permitted me to include the story here in his own words.

What the Heck Came Through Here?

It was going to be a pretty low-key fishing/camping trip. I always go alone, fish all night, and return in the morning. But this time was different. I was bringing along my wife and five-year-old. My wife Vicky's idea of camping is the Holiday Inn and my little girl, Abby, is just beginning to appreciate insects, river mud, and the great outdoors. I packed my three fishing poles and one bait pole. We camped along the side of the great Missouri River. During that afternoon and evening we enjoyed some small catches, and

Abby pulled in a 3-pound flathead. As the sun began to set, I put my fishing poles out. Two of the poles had 1-pound Drum and one pole was baited with a 6-inch channel catfish. Why catfish for bait? I always go after big cats, and big cats will eat smaller cats. I don't get big cats often, but when I do it makes up for all of the nights of no big cats. Knowing what a big cat can do to a fishing pole, I tied up all three poles with rope and tied them off to a log. Since I had bells on my poles, I would know if I got any bites.

It was 11:00 P.M., and my wife and daughter were snug in the back of my Blazer, but no room for me. I slept beside, and my poles were about 75 feet away. At 4:00 A.M. I was awakened to a violent sound of a set of bells being ripped back and forth. I thought to myself, "That's a 50-pound-plus on the line." I got up, and of the three fishing poles, my middle pole was gone! All that could be seen was a rope dipping into the river. I gently pulled the rope and retrieved my pole. I carefully untied the pole from the rope, knowing what was probably in store. I reeled very slowly, taking all slack out of the line. I then set the hook, and the fight was on. Line was stripping off of the reel, screaming as something massive was making its way out to the channel. I finally got it turned around and reeling the massive fish in toward shore. I fought this heavy and powerful creature for about twenty minutes, but had no idea how big—or what—the creature was. As I got it toward shore, I grew more concerned I would lose him as I tried to get him into shore. And don't you know, I did not bring my large dip net. If I'm with my wife and daughter, just how much fishing would I get done anyway? On my first try pulling him in toward shore, he peeled off another 20 yards of line. He was not ready to give up this fight. And it is very easy to lose a big cat as it is approaching the shore. He could snap my 30-pound test line pretty easy. After a few more minutes, I tired him out, and as I got him to shore, I could not believe just how big this cat was. I waded out about 3 feet, put one hand in his mouth, and clamped on to his jaw; then he clamped down on my hand, and his tail violently shook the water. I honestly thought he would dislocate my shoulder. I threw my fishing pole on shore and used my other hand to grab his jaw, and quickly pulled him to shore. What a catch, and what a fight. I tied him up and surprised my wife and daughter. But there is more. As I went to check on my other two poles, both lines had been broken by something else. Both poles had a 1-pound Drum for bait, and both poles had a broken line. Just exactly what came through here? Two large gars? It is unknown to this day. But one thing for sure: You never know when the big one will strike, so be prepared. It could happen to you tonight! And take your wife and kids camping. A pretty good luck charm, wouldn't you say?

My Comment: Rick's fishing stories always have a happy ending. He always practices the catch and release policy, and this big one he released weighed 75 pounds and is just hanging around his favorite fishing hole, waiting to get even with Rick.

About the fisherman: Rick Olsen is a retired Army Officer who resides in Leavenworth, Kansas. He teaches Military Leadership at the Command & General Staff College, Fort Leavenworth, Kansas. He fishes often and loves to fish and camp all night, targeting big cats.

Part 2

Leaving Kansas and Moving On

Building a Personal Bridge
from Kansas to Michigan

I had a job that I liked and had no intention of changing jobs until a friend told me that the company he was working for was looking for someone to hire. It was for the same job he had, but in a different state. His title was District Sales Manager.

The company was the Stran Steel Building division of the fifth largest steel manufacturing company in the country, National Steel Corporation.

I met with the National Sales Manager based in Detroit and another man who was the Regional Sales Manager based in Minneapolis at the airport in Kansas City. They listened to me try to sell myself into one of their job openings. I told them I did not have much experience in selling, but I said I knew steel and what you can do with it and what you can't do with it. That must have caught their attention, and later I realized they had no idea what I was talking about.

This meeting occurred in the early summer and was followed up with a similar meeting with a sales engineer based in Washington, DC at the same airport in Kansas City. He was looking for a sales engineer to be based in Chicago, Illinois. I told him the same thing I said to the previous people, only he knew what I was talking about.

I had no more contact with any of them until mid-September. They were interested in me but could not commit to a definite time-schedule then.

Meanwhile, back at my regular job I was called to a meeting with the Vice President and his sales manager. They told me they wanted to promote me to a selling and estimating position. It would be a good raise in pay and a great opportunity for advancement.

It was very hard to say, but I had to turn them down. When the V. P. asked me when I was leaving, I told him thirty days. He said, "Thirty days it is," and left the room. Fortunately for me, in thirty days I had left Kansas and was on my way to the Stran headquarters located in Ecorse, Michigan, just outside of Detroit.

At that point everything happened quickly. I met the National Sales Manager again, and he took me to the Executive Dining Room for lunch. I then spent two days of indoctrination, flew first-class on a dinner flight to Washington, and checked in to the grand, old Lafayette Hotel just a block or two from the White House.

Then for the next few weeks I went daily to the Washington office of the Architectural Product Division. This was the name for the promotion and selling of light gage steel that was to replace wood members in housing that forbade flammable materials.

I spent this time doing simple drawing, some little design problems, and new product familiarization. I think they just wanted to see if I knew which end to sharpen my wooden pencils.

By Christmas time I had a new job title, Zone Sales Engineer, and my own office in Des Plains, Illinois, just north of the airport in Chicago. I shared a secretary with the separate Metal Building employees and traveled fourteen mid-western states from Ohio to Montana by air. In Kansas, my boss was two drawing boards behind me, now my nearest boss was in Washington, DC, some 700 miles away.

It was a good association for me, and I stayed in Chicago for about two years. I filled in for an empty position in Rapid City, South Dakota for a short time and then transferred to Lansing, Michigan, working with the Metal Building Division under the new company name, National Steel Products.

I retired from there after twenty years.

Doe Night

When I first came to Michigan, one of the first people I had to call upon was a metal building contractor named Bernard Card. My company was selling under a franchise type of business, and Bernard was always one of our nationally-ranked sales leaders. My predecessor was a second-generation Albanian with a slight accent that seemed a little odd to Mr. Card, a native-born Canadian. He expected a little more from Mr. Card than Mr. Card was willing to provide, and I replaced him. My accent was a little more to his liking, and my love for the outdoors was something we shared. It built into a lifelong friendship. I used to tell him, "I've only been up here a few years, and now I talk the same as yo'all do, eh?"

Mr. Card owned an 80 acre wooded tract of prime hunting land outside of Rose City, Michigan, that he used primarily for deer hunting. On this land he built a pond and a modern log cabin used for entertaining customers with cook-outs and family gatherings and parties, etc. He often had presidents or top management people there as his guests trying to persuade them to come to his town, build their factories, and hire the local people.

He, in turn, would serve as the general contractor for the project, and buy and erect a metal building shell through me. He was very successful at this.

His land was heavily wooded, and there was a road on the perimeter of it. He built six or eight deer blinds with all the modern conveniences, like an office chair to swivel around in to enlarge the field of fire from deer rifles, and a small propane stove to keep one's coffee and donuts warm during the cool, frosty fall mornings.

The buildings were about 5' x 5' with hinged openings at setting shoulder height and had thin sheet metal sides and roof to protect from the weather. If one should fire a high-powered rifle with the tip of the barrel still inside the blind, instead of sticking the barrel outside, one would be subjected to a very loud reverberating blast that could deafen you for the remainder of the day—and awaken people from miles around.

One day, Mr. Card had just finished a very encouraging meeting at his office with a potential customer who was looking for a town in which to build a new plant. The visitor required an available labor force and a successful, honest local contractor who had design and building capabilities. Both of these requirements were fields in which Mr. Card excelled.

Although not the president of his company, the young man had a very responsible position. He would make the decision as to where the new plant would be built and who would build it.

He was staying in town for the night, and when their meeting was finished, Mr. Card asked him if he would have dinner and a drink. The young man agreed, and Mr. Card produced a bottle of bourbon from his desk. They then proceeded to talk deer season and hunting in general.

One of the things they discussed was the strictly-enforced hunting laws and bag limits. For instance, at that time they were in a buck-only area, and severe penalties were enforced if one were to shoot a doe white-tailed deer. Most of the area hunters were non-local people, and the local game warden was very unforgiving if he should catch a game violator from downstate.

My old friend Dr. Sorenson back in Kansas, when I related to him the $1,000 fine imposed on a violator for shooting a doe out of season, said, "The fine was not enough. They should forget the money, and make him eat the whole deer." Thankfully, this opinion is not shared by everyone.

So Mr. Card invited the young businessman out to his hunting land to have dinner. He sent his grown son and a friend of his to buy some steaks, go out to the cabin, open it up, and start a fire to prepare the meal. In the meantime, Mr. Card and his guest finished their drinks and took a tour around the town.

They visited the new industrial park, noted available housing for key company people, and then took a back road to the hunting land. When they reached the cabin right at twilight, they watched as a flock of wild turkeys came out to feed at a feeding station Mr. Card kept available to them year round.

The four men had an enjoyable dinner and sat around talking hunting and outdoor sporting in general for a couple of hours. Mr. Card then offered to drive around the land, see some of the blinds, and maybe a deer. The invitation was agreeable, though Mr. Card's son and his friend declined to join in and drove away.

When they left, Mr. Card said he had forgot something, and returned carrying his deer rifle. He said the place was pretty remote and deer season was only a couple of days away, and that sometimes if they could find a nice young doe they would take her as a camp deer.

This seemed very odd to the young man after all the talk about game violators and penalties, but he refrained from commenting. They drove around with Mr. Card acting like a tour guide, noting the various blinds and who would hunt there opening day.

At one point, now dark, Mr. Card slowed the pickup and rolled down the window very quietly. He said he thought he saw what he was looking for, and picked up the rifle. He told the man to come around to the back of the truck, which he did.

Mr. Card tried to point out a doe, but the young man could not quite make her out. Mr. Card said he would put the rifle's scope on her, and when he did, he pulled the trigger and shot the rifle. In such a setting, early on a quiet fall evening, the noise was deafening.

At this point, he said he was pretty sure he got her, asked the young man to hold the rifle, and hurried out into the darkness after the deer. He had not been gone thirty seconds before the sound of an engine revving up was heard, and across an open field a flashing red light was rapidly approaching with a siren blaring into the night.

All the young man could think of was the severe punishment given game violators in this area. There was a doe shot in a buck-only area. It was dark and after legal shooting hours. The hunting season had not yet started. He did not have a hunting license and he had a smoking gun in his hand.

He could see big-time fines coming, maybe even some jail time. The only thing to do was to move out fast and after running about 50 yards he realized he held a just-fired rifle in his hands. Logic said to get rid of the smoking gun, and he threw the gun away. More logic: He didn't know where he was running to, and he did not do anything wrong. Only one thing to do: go back to the pickup and face the music.

He wearily walked back to the pickup, prepared to fight for his innocence. When he got back he was greeted by a smiling Mr. Card, his son, and his son's friend. Both of the young men were volunteer firemen, and the flashing red light and a siren were on their personal pickup.

At that moment the young man was extremely relieved and too happy to be angry, and enjoyed the joke played on him. Later perhaps he might not be so happy.

Afterwards Mr. Card asked where the rifle was. The young man asked what direction he had come from, and when they told him, he said to go in that direction about 50 yards, and there he had thrown the gun about 15 yards to the right. His directions were accurate, but they had to come back the next morning to find the rifle.

Mr. Card was very civic-minded. He helped establish a local Lions Club, but the local members soon learned about his sense of humor.

At one of the monthly meetings he held a raffle to raise funds. When the winning ticket was selected for a washer and dryer, and the winner was awarded a wash cloth and a towel, everybody laughed except the winner.

When the next raffle was held, people still bought tickets,

primarily just to see what was forthcoming. The winning ticket was drawn for a garbage disposal, and when the box was carried out by two men and opened, the winner was surprised to find a tiny live pig.

Great joke, but the winner would not take the pig home, nor would anyone else at the meeting, and the president was stuck with tending a baby pig.

There was a serious side as well to the local Lions Club. The funds they received were spent on the formation of an ambulance service. Not only did they run the service from a new ambulance, but the local members staffed the service too. Several members were on call around the clock, and several personal phone lines would ring at the same time when service was needed. This filled a great need for emergency service since the closest hospital was small and some distance away in West Branch, Michigan.

Bernard Card has passed on, but has a wife, four sons, one daughter, many grandchildren, and many friends to keep his memory alive.

Personal Reflection: Whitetail deer hunting can be very exciting, especially if the first deer to appear is within the possibility of making a clean kill. Some hunters get so nervous that they cannot hold the gun steady. Others cannot manage to pull the trigger. I know of one man who was given the opportunity to make a clean kill on a fake deer, but he could not pull the trigger of his rifle. When handed a rifle belonging to his host he made a clean kill shot. Then he walked up to the supposedly dead deer and found it was not a deer at all. He was so ashamed, mad, disappointed and embarrassed, that he walked back to his host's car without saying another word. They drove back to the lodge where the guest picked up his wife, loaded all their hunting gear in his own car, and left the camp without saying goodbye.

Needless to say, it was one potential customer who was no longer a customer. Sometimes when hunters are successful bagging a deer year after year, they become forgetful what that first deer meant to them and what it means to novice hunters. This happened to be this elderly gentleman's first deer.

Midnight Wolves

I have known Randy Martin for a long time. He was mostly a speaking acquaintance, but when I began to hear stories about his bear hunting, and since I was in the process of writing a new book, I had to get to know him better. I thought those stories, if true, would be a natural for inclusion in the book. Not only were they true, he graciously granted me permission to use them, and spent time with me to get down all the facts that I needed.

Randy and his wife Sue are second-generation wild bear hunting enthusiasts and keep a kennel of hunting hounds that they breed primarily for their own use.

They have perfected a line of dogs with enough grit and stamina to hunt bear. This bloodline reaches back some sixty years when Julius Sebastian, Sue's father, started the Sebastian Blues line with registered Bluetick hounds. Randy and Sue keep frozen semen from some of their great hounds dating back some twenty years.

They are both retired now and spend a good amount of time during the fall months hunting the woodlands.

We hear occasionally from people who are trying to get you to adopt a pet, and it's said that when you have a pet you are obligated to take care it for its lifetime. This is especially true if you are a wild bear hunter and have your own hunting hounds. These dogs are actually putting their life in jeopardy for you when chasing and fighting wild bears.

Some bear hunts are ended very quickly. A young or smaller bear will choose to take refuge in a tree. But if a bear is very large, he will probably prefer to stay on the ground and run away from the hounds. The hounds invariably catch up with the bear, and a serious life or death fight begins with the hounds surrounding it. The bear fights the dogs with long, slashing claws and sharp teeth, and sometimes seriously injures or kills the hounds.

If the fight is prolonged, and the hunter's favorite dogs are being injured and all the movement will not let the hunter get a clear shot at the bear, the hunter will decide to get into the fight himself. This move to get in close to assist the dogs and get a clear shot at the fighting bear is not recommended for most hunters.

Bears are usually very shy of humans, and when the hunting dogs catch up to the fleeing bear and the fight begins, it usually lasts until the hunter approaches. Most of the time the bear runs away until the dogs catch up with it again, and round two begins.

This chase and fight sequence can last for many hours, especially if the terrain is very rough and the dogs cannot keep up with the fleeing bear. Then is the time the hunter needs to get to his wounded dogs as soon as possible and perform whatever medical attention he can give. This is where radio collars are used to locate each wounded—or just plain lost—dog. The hunter and the trucks also have radio collars to help find the way back when the hunt is over.

The wounded dogs are transported back to camp and medical first aid is administered. A seriously wounded dog can often require $1,000 in veterinary surgery and hospital costs. Some hunters carry their own first aid kits and are adept at applying sutures and treating other battlefield type injuries.

Most of the time when bear hunting one would assume the bear is acting in the role of self defense, but occasionally a bear will be encountered who is exceptionally mean and seems to delight in the destruction of bear dogs.

During a hunt in Wisconsin a fighting bear was found when a bunch of hunters had pooled their hounds and started a chase. Before the hunt was over, a total of fourteen hounds had been disabled. Randy Martin's personal medical veterinary bills totaled over $2,000 for this one-day's hunt.

Sassy was one of Randy's most promising young dogs, and she failed to show up with the other hounds one day at the end of a hunt. The hunt had been in very rough country with steep hills and swamp that made the dog's radio collar signal very weak; sometimes with no signal at all.

Randy searched for two days with no luck finding the dog, but they had the approximate location of the signal. Randy, knowing the dog may still be alive and wounded or lost, felt obligated to find out for sure. He decided to try to find the dog at night when the radio signal might be a bit louder.

They were hunting in Upper Michigan's Baraga County in an area known as the Sturgeon River Gorge. This is a large area with few roads, and almost impassable for humans. The radio signal on Sassy's collar was coming from deep within this gorge.

The next night, long after sundown, Randy and a fellow hunter (who reluctantly accompanied him) left camp to find the dog. They drove to the beginning of the gorge where they immediately picked up a much stronger signal from Sassy's collar, and he felt he was close to finding the dog.

They left the truck and had not gone a hundred yards when surprisingly they heard wolves howling in the distance, and they seemed to be coming closer. At this point, Randy's companion decided that it would be safer if he waited in the pick-up so he would be where the radio was more readily available to summon assistance if need be.

Both men knew that the endangered Gray Wolves had been successfully introduced in Michigan, but did not know of any wolves in the Sturgeon River Gorge area.

Randy walked into the pitch black night all alone, knowing this may be the last chance to find Sassy. As he walked through the swamp and downed trees, the sound of wolves seemed to be coming closer.

Since he thought he might be carrying a wounded dog back with him, he did not take along his heavy rifle. He did have his very powerful Smith & Wesson .41 Magnum pistol though. Other than the gun, all he had on him was the hunting light on his cap and his radio collar which was set to match the location of the collar he had just left hanging on the truck's exterior rearview mirror.

As the radio signal grew louder he began to hear the howling of wolves again in the distance. By the time he got to the dog collar's maximum radio sound, there were three wolves howling close to him. One wolf was following Randy's trail, one was on the left side of him, with the third on the right keeping pace with his movements.

The collar signal area was a flat sandy place that was overgrown with shoulder high weeds and large boulders scattered throughout. He climbed on top of one of the boulders to better see with the hunting light he had turned on when he picked up the signal, yet no sign of the missing dog. He thought maybe she had lost her collar and was still loose somewhere in the area, but no dog or collar could be found.

He decided to go back to the truck with the intent of coming back the next day for a more thorough search in daylight. With the wolves still howling, he walked the half a mile to the safety of the truck. When he neared the truck he heard a dog bark. The bark they give when they are lost. The lost bark. He had found Sassy, and she was in trouble and calling him for help.

That was all he needed. He walked back the distance to the collar location and climbed the same big rock overlooking the collar area. He saw weeds moving toward him and was convinced it was Sassy. When he called to her the weeds stopped moving, and soon after the wolves stopped howling. He knew it was time to leave. He did now know if the wolves had left or were merely lying in wait for him as he made his way back out of the gorge.

So, it's 1:00 A.M. and he is one half mile from his truck. He is surrounded by at least three wolves, and he has that feeling you get when you are alone in the deep woods at night. He could almost imagine a wolf lying behind every tree waiting to pounce on him. His big pistol wouldn't be much help against three wolves, and I am sure he had never felt so all alone in his life.

Walking over downed trees and through swamp land is very dangerous even in daylight, but at night he could be in big trouble. What if he happened to sprain an ankle or the battery in his homing device didn't function properly, or the spare dog collar radio that was hooked on the exterior rearview mirror of the truck had come loose and fallen off when driven over rough roads?

He was able to make it back to the truck without harm, and since he had finally located the lost collar radio area, he and his wife decided to visit the site in daylight in a last look to find out what happened to Sassy.

The next day they made the long walk back through the woods and swamp to the big rock. After a thorough look all through the weeds there was no trace of the dog or the collar. They finally gave up and started to walk away.

Although the ground was firm and sandy, when Randy's wife stepped on something that did not feel just right, she looked down and saw something that showed a few brown hairs. She called out to Randy. When he reached down and moved the sand, he found Sassy's head covered up with the radio collar still attached and still sending out radio signals.

When he gave the collar a jerk to pull her body out of the sand, only the head and collar came. The body was not attached. Apparently the dog had been killed and eaten, and only the head remained buried in the sandy soil.

When Randy took the dog's head to the local office of the Department of National Resources for identification and to determine what kind of animal had killed the dog, he was able to talk to one of the men who had the responsibility of introducing the wolf pack into the gorge. He was told the place where they found the dog was used as a rendezvous area where the young wolves were kept in safety while the mature wolves were hunting at night. The mature wolves would then bring back food for the young ones.

Apparently Randy had arrived at the rendezvous site a few moments before the pack returned to pick up the young wolf cubs, and the pack found him there waiting for them. I would bet the wolves shadowed Randy all the way back to the waiting truck.

When Randy took the dog's head to the head of the Rose Lake Game Management area outside of Lansing, he took one look at it and said, "Wolf kill."

It was at this point that Randy decided no more big handguns at night for defense against packs of wolves; it would be shotguns and buckshot.

Flies Ain't the Only Way

Clare was one of my business friends who had his office located in a very classy office building in the riot, burned-out section of north East Detroit. His was the only office in use in his city block, or perhaps several blocks around.

He was a professional engineer and president of a general contracting corporation that bought metal buildings from me. He had only one fault. He was the ultimate fly fisherman. In the caste system of fishermen, only top-water plug fishermen spoke to him, and he spoke fishoneese only to God.

One afternoon, after business hours, when we were trying to shake off the after-effects of a two-martini lunch, we were swapping fishing tales at one of Detroit's finest establishments. After listening to Clare about his upcoming yearly trek to go fly-fishing, by bush plane that is, to the eastern shore of Saint James Bay in Northern Canada, naturally I decided to express my comparable fishing experiences in—yes, in—Big Stranger Creek, just outside of Easton, Kansas, about forty miles northwest of Kansas City, Kansas.

But first he told me about the bush plane on pontoons that flew him and his two partners to their campsite far away from civilization. They had to take all their food for a three week stay with only a radio for contact in an emergency, and they had their own canoe strapped to the pontoons. They had a large number of fly-fishing rods and numerous boxes of home-tied flies. Plus all their clothes, including rain gear and extensive first aid kits.

They also had their big bottles of duty-free alcohol to be used only for medicinal purposes such as a black fly or mosquito bite, and their big hunting knives on the left side of their belts in a right-handed cross draw, if they needed the knife in a hurry. And they had a big gorilla mask.

I heard of one group of fly-in anglers who, unbelievably, had excess bottles of liquor that they did not want to take back through customs at the U.S. border, so they decided to bury the bottles to be retrieved on their next annual trip. This is a practice they carried on for many years, and they never were able to remember the burial sites or retrieve any of the buried bottles.

After listening dutifully about the distances traveled and the total cost of the flights to the fishing camp and back, I decided he should be privileged to hear about our much simpler and easier way to land some big fish. I told him the equipment was simple, and everybody was always equipped and ready to go. Actually, the only equipment required was a good, tight baseball cap, a pair of worn-out tennis shoes, and a pair of (preferably old) bib overalls. At this point I could see a bit of disbelief in Clare's eyes, but he was clearly eager to hear the rest of the story.

Big Stranger Creek runs through farmland for most of its length, but it does pass through a few small towns and has been known to flood all the bottom land as lately as the spring of 2007. As far as I remember, the stream is from 30-to-40 feet wide and some 4 feet deep, with much deeper holes where the stream goes around a bend in the creek.

There are a lot of trees, dead and alive, lining the banks with their roots extending into the water, which gives haven to flathead catfish. Some of these fish can be as big as seventy-five pounds, and of course a lot smaller ones.

The creek is usually muddy, so it's hard to see when you are immersed in the water, and the only way to catch the fish is to get in the water, duck your head into it next to the tree roots, and feel for a fish resting there.

When you feel the fish, and it is one you want, you have to rub, or tickle, his back to soothe him. Then you feel for his mouth, and when he opens it to expel water through his gills for oxygen, you grab his lower jaw, pull him out, and throw him out on the bank.

Unfortunately, the larger the fish, the more reluctantly they object to leaving the water. And if you happen to grab a 50-to-75 pound fish by the mouth, it soon becomes obvious to all that it's not clear whether the fisherman has caught a fish or a fish has caught a fisherman. Because now the fisherman is spending half the time under water, and he is primarily concerned how to get loose, and, secondly, how to get help landing the fish.

I could see now, that Clare is mentally putting himself under water holding the big fish and wondering what comes next—and what about the baseball cap and the bib overalls?

I told him that with all the water splashing, the creek bank, which is sometimes pretty steep, gets wet, and one could lose one's footing. This is why it's really good to have a buddy along up on the bank. But he could have trouble getting into the battle to help and needs something to grab onto to pull the two combatants out of the water. The closest thing he could grab onto of the fisherman is his hair.

Now a when really big fish is caught this way and will not let go of the hand, and if the fisherman's buddy is big and strong, the natural inclination is to grab the fisherman by the hair to pull them up. Some people strongly object to being pulled out of the water by their hair, and it could make them lose their grip on the fish's mouth. It's also rumored that losing great patches of one's hair this way could lead to premature incidents of male pattern baldness. Hence the baseball caps.

The simple alternative: The fisherman must wear a pair of bib overalls with the wide straps over the shoulders. They make an acceptable option to hold on to rather than the hair pull. This alternative is preferable unless the buddy on the bank is a weightlifter, sport aficionado, and is aware of the "pull-and-jerk" option. This violet movement might be harmful to other anatomical locations on the fisherman, and should be discussed before the fisherman gets into the water.

For most fishermen, the larger the catch, the better. A big fish taken will get your name in the local paper, the *Leavenworth Times*, and a really big fish will get your picture in the paper. Recently I found out that catching fish this way is now illegal in Stranger Creek, so every name and picture in the paper has a description of the imaginary bait, line strength used, etc., to keep the local game warden from knocking on their door.

This story happened a long time ago, so I thought that I had better check the Fishing Regulations in Kansas and found that the name "Hogging Catfish" is no longer acceptable. It now has a new hi-tech name: "Hand Fishing."

"Hand Fishing" is permissible only in two rivers, in certain areas in Kansas, and definitely illegal in Stranger Creek. Sorry, Clare.

I am still waiting for fishing laws to be mailed to me because I did not like what I read on-line about the fishing regulations that stated, "No manmade objects such as *barrels, boxes, or bath tubs* may be used attract fish." Only the yellow flathead catfish can be caught this way.

Now I find myself like Clare, imagining being under water and holding a big fish. Not good. The image of me cramming my tall 6' 6" of humanity into a 5 foot bathtub with a fifty pound, totally ticked-off catfish violently thrashing and whipsawing the back of my hand raw with his rough sandpaper jaws, is not something I want to think about or would like to do on a regular basis. In fact, I do not think I will do it for the first time.

Not too long ago, I was sitting as a guest at the bar in the local Eagles Club in Leavenworth, waiting to get into a Schafkopf card game, and got into a discussion with two big full-grown men about Hogging Catfish.

They both proclaimed there is no way they would participate in this sport. They said what if when feeling under the tree roots you found a snapping turtle that could bite your finger off…or maybe a poisonous water moccasin or rattlesnake. Sometimes when the creek goes around a bend the water is much deeper, and what if the fish took you into deep water and would not let you go. Or maybe you could get tangled up in the tree roots and could not get loose. Consensus: No thanks. We will read it in the paper.

Clare said he would not particularly like to try the catfish fishing, and I am sure the people in the bar would not like to be dropped off with two companions for a three-week stay on St. James Bay. Me? I just talk about these things, and write some of them down.

So, I have lost contact with Clare after all these years, but I'll bet he is still going up to St. James Bay. And I'll bet he is still wearing the gorilla mask as he travels up I-75 to Canada, sitting in the passenger's seat trying to frighten people in their cars that they pass along the way.

Cadillac Bear

There is an old saying in competitive situations: "Sometimes you eat the bear, and sometimes the bear eats you." This came close to happening to my good friend, Randy Martin. You probably heard of someone big enough and bad enough to go bear hunting with a switch. Well, Randy found himself bear hunting without a switch—or a gun. He only had his bare hands and one bear hound on a leash.

The Black Bear hunting season in Michigan starts in middle-September and lasts for some thirty days. You would naturally think that this particular day's hunt would have occurred in Michigan's Upper Peninsula where ninety percent of the bear population lived. But it happened in the middle of the state on public land near the city of Cadillac. This is a great area for summer homes and vacationers with many good fishing lakes and a limited bear population.

Fortunately, this incident occurred after Labor Day, and with the opening of the fall school terms most of the summer people and the vacationers had returned to their homes.

Randy, after taking a bear the day before, decided to accompany, along with his dogs, a local guide who had been hired by other hunters who had failed to show up in time for a hunt. A young man, a friend of the guide whom Randy did not know, would accompany them as a hunter.

Now, when Randy goes into the woods in bear season he usually carries a Smith & Wesson .41 Caliber Magnum pistol for his own protection. But today the guide leading the hunt said he was not comfortable with anyone carrying a handgun other than himself and would appreciate it if Randy would leave his gun in the cabin. Naturally, Randy did.

His particular model is one of the most powerful handguns available. It weighs close to three pounds, fires a 210 grain bullet, and has a muzzle velocity of 1.600 feet per second. It is more than strong enough to stop a bear with a decent shot location, and is almost as powerful as the Magnum 44 used in the "Dirty Harry" movies.

This hunt started on public land that bordered private land and was separated by a seldom-traveled macadam road with shallow ditches on both sides. They intended to make every effort to keep the bear from crossing it and to keep the hunting away from private homes just across the road.

They had not been in the woods long before the dogs picked up the scent of a bear, and the chase began. They caught a glimpse of the bear and were amazed at its huge size. After chasing it in large circles through blown-down trees and swamps for some three hours, they were not surprised when it headed toward the road, and the private land and houses on the other side.

One of the guide's young dogs was misbehaving, could not be controlled, and would not stay with the guide's pack of hounds. Since Randy was just an observer that day, he was given the chore of holding onto the young dog with a leash—if he could catch him. He was to drive ahead of the hunt, stand on the road, and try to keep the bear from crossing until the dogs and the hunters caught up with the fleeing bear.

At this point it was decided that the young man should accompany Randy in the truck and get ahead of the hunt.

Randy stood on the road where he thought the bear might cross, and the young hunter stood about one hundred yards further up the road with a .30-06 deer rifle waiting for it to cross. Hunting with a young person you have never met before and who is carrying a high-powered rifle makes one nervous. The bear may cross the road between the two of you, and the guy may decide to shoot in your direction.

As they waited, the guide's young dog that had been misbehaving and would not stay with guide's pack of hounds, decided he would hunt with Randy. It joined him and did not object to being tied to a leach.

Randy and the dog took up position on the far side of the road. Hopefully, should a bear come their way in an attempt to cross the road, he could shout and wave at it. Bears are normally very shy of humans, and he felt confident he could turn the bear back into the woods.

The heavy woods ended about one hundred yards from

the road, and waist-high ground cover continued to the edge of a shallow ditch that ran along the edge. Randy could hear the dogs in the woods, and when the chase reached the ground cover, he could see the dogs jumping above the weeds, trying to see the bear. The dogs could hear and smell it, but were not close enough to see the bear and were jumping like kittens playing with a mouse. Getting too close to the bear in these weeds could put them within reach of the long teeth and three-inch slashing claws of the bear.

Randy saw the bear at the same time the bear saw Randy and the dog barking from across the ditch and the bear started running right to by-pass them. Randy waved his arms and shouted, and with the dogs, ran to the right to meet the bear who, when he saw them, immediately ran back the other direction, still in the ditch along the road, to again meet the running Randy and the dog. This happened one more time.Now the bear had enough, and from about twenty feet away the bear decided that if he could not get around Randy and the dog, he would just go through them—and he charged the unarmed man!

So this is what they had on the road: One fleeing bear, three baying hounds fighting the bear, one young hunter with a rifle in his hands (with the safety off and his finger on the trigger starting to point down the road), and one unarmed hunter with only a noncombatant Bluetick hound on a leash.

So here comes a fighting-mad bear. Randy was in the field for the first time without his very powerful handgun and promised himself this would be the last time. He knew he could not run away from the bear. And one dog would not put up much of a fight, particularly if he was hampered by a leash.

There was only one thing to do. He picked up the baying dog. By this time the bear is only about 8 feet away. He threw the dog up in the air at the bear. The bear immediately skidded to a stop and ducked his head to avoid the dog (which landed over the bear's head on his crouching shoulders). This gave Randy and the dog time to briskly move out.

Apparently the bear had enough distraction and continued his original path as fast as possible, ignoring both the Bluetick hound and Randy. The young man did not fire his rifle. He remained a cheering observer and rejoined the hunt.

I do not know what the bear was thinking. Perhaps he was afraid of being so close to Randy and the dog. But I'm inclined to believe he did not mind the men or all the baying dogs that were chasing him. What he did not know about—and was not prepared for—was being dive-bombed in an air attack by the Bluetick Hound Dog Air Force!

I have not played golf with Randy lately, but I have been told by others that he has a slight twitch in his trigger finger when lining up a long putt if the wind makes a slight noise blowing through the leaves behind him.

Note: This bear was taken later in the day on private land by a different hunter after a four hour chase. The dogs chased the bear right up to a man hunting over a bait pile who shot the bear. The bear weighed 456 pounds.

Fox Hound

We had a deer hunting camp in Northern Lower Michigan with 1300 acres of mostly cedar swampland.

Our leased area was natural habitat for Black Bears. We had one local member named Charley Schaar who was an avid bear hunter, and he had several Blue Tic and Plott hunting hounds.

Charley had just returned from a long weekend trip to the mountainous area of east Tennessee seeking a new dog to improve his breeding stock, and he came home with a yet unnamed, good-looking new hound.

Not long after he returned, Charley was in the field with a number of buddies who also had hounds, and they were all working their dogs to get them in physical shape for the upcoming bear hunting season. At this time, one could chase bears with the dogs but could not harm them until the season opened later in the fall.

One afternoon they were returning from an extra-long chase, and they were not able to get all the hounds together. Long after dark, they finally arrived back to where they had started out with the dogs.

Charley had problems keeping his new hound under control and was the last man to return with the new hound held on a leash. When Charley reached the rendezvous point he found his friends sitting on the tailgates of their pickups with the headlights turned on and drinking beer out of cans with all the bear hounds lying on the ground resting around them. They were all waiting for Charley so they could get the trucks loaded and go home.

Charley, who at this point was not in the mood for pleasantries, actually turned down an offer of a cold can of beer and decided to load his dog in the box in the back of the pickup and depart for home.

Each of the pickups had a wooden box in the back with a large door in the side to keep the dogs in for safety when riding to and from the hunting site, and Charley was teaching the new dog to go into the box on command. But this night the dog was reluctant to enter the box.

What Charley did not know was that his friends had

captured a live raccoon and put it in Charley's dog box. At this point everyone, men and dogs, knew about the coon except Charley and his new hound.

Charley, being tired from his strenuous day job of teaching school, decided a little more force was needed. He squatted down behind the dog, grabbed the dog's collar with one hand and his tail by the other hand, and was going to throw the dog through the open door in the box.

At this point, with the dog's nose in the box, the raccoon made a large screaming growl and lunged at the dog. The dog yelped, and since Charley's nose was also near the door in the box, the noise more than startled him too!

At the noise, Charley started to stand up just as the frightened dog lunged backwards to get away from the coon. It struck Charley in the middle of his chest knocking him head-over-heels backwards out the back of the truck and onto the ground with the dog falling on top of him.

He held onto the dog's collar because he did not want to spend the rest of the night trying to catch a runaway dog. The dog did not like what was happening and decided he would give Charley a little nip on his hand (not his good hand, but the one that the chain saw split between the second and third fingers not too long ago), and he was free.

When Charley got around to using language more appropriate for a high school English teacher, he looked for his dog, and there was Mr. Field Dog Stud Book, future surefire grand-champion, coon-fearing bear hound about15 feet away wagging his tail.

I think the dog stood there watching because he had never seen anyone get out of a pickup that way. When the ruckus started with the raccoon, all the other baying dogs jumped into the pickup at once and hopped around trying to get the coon out of the box. But there was no way Charley's dog was going to get up there with those crazy mutts.

You could almost see what it was thinking. What is the matter with those idiots? Can't they see I am a foxhound, and we chase those little red animals, not too fast, but just enough for the bosses to hear our voices, and then let the foxes get to safety in their holes in the ground?

In the meantime, the men are not running around in the swamp in the middle of the night. They just built a nice comfortable fire on a hilltop and sit or lay around it with some homemade sipping whisky, and maybe even have a nice little nap. They just listen to the foxhounds sing, and about ten-thirty they blow their cow horns and they all go home.

Trying to chase an animal that outweighs me by about twenty-five times, has long sharp teeth, longer claws and would like to have me for its supper, is not something a normal foxhound would relish. And what about the pickup lights turned on and the canned beer in the middle of the night? And they call *us* rednecks?

Now that Charley could see the dog was not going to run away, he still had to face all that laughter from his fellow hunters, along with the truckload of baying hounds and the live coon in the back of his pickup.

He jumped into the bed of his truck and started grabbing dogs and throwing them out. He kept the last dog, grabbing the $1,000 bear dog, much to the owners chagrin, and threw it into the box with the live raccoon!

Had it been a much older raccoon in such a confined area it was possible the dog could have been killed, but it wasn't hurt. The owner, however, did have a few anxious moments before he got his dog out of the box, and then the show was over.

They all went home with the foxhound sitting up boldly in his new permanent seat, the passenger's side of Charley's pickup, no doubt watching in the headlights for bears on the sides of the road.

Wolf Skin

The following story may be a little bit too gruesome for inclusion in this book. Although most of the book is about wild game killing of animals—fish and fowl—it was all done with the idea that the kills were for human consumption.

The state of Michigan re-introduced packs of Gray Wolves into the wilds of the Upper Peninsula, and they have multiplied very successfully to everyone's satisfaction, except for some of the local people who consider them a threat to livestock and the white-tailed deer herd and people who are very wary of them.

Even some deer hunters do not trust the animals with just cause. One of my good friends, David Parish, was hunting with his son when the young man shot and fatally wounded a white-tailed deer. Rather than immediately follow the deer and take a chance on the deer running a great distance from the blind, they decided to take a break for lunch and then follow the tracks, hoping the deer did not run too far away from the blind. Hand carrying a slain deer through heavy woods, downed timber, or swamp is one of the more unpleasant chores sometimes required for a successful deer hunt.

When they finished lunch they followed the tracks in the snow for a short distance and found the dead deer. What they found though was not the making of a fine trophy to be remembered as the young man's first kill, but a half-eaten and fought-over carcass—and hundreds of wolf tracks. The find was only about a hundred yards from their cabin, and it made them consider the possibility of a human wolf attack.

It was the first snow of the season, and they had no idea there were wolves in their hunting area. They could not feel safe now just walking outside the cabin at night without a gun, knowing they may well be under surveillance by some of the wolves. Their cabin was in a very isolated part of the woods, and they were not sure now if a bagged deer hanging on a buck pole would still be there the next morning.

I do not know of anyone who has seen a pack of wolves attacking and killing a prey. I would assume it would resemble the television productions on African wildlife programs showing the feeding frenzy of a pride of lions or pack of wild dogs or hyenas.

The following is a description of what happened during this last season of bear hunting in the Sturgeon River Gorge area in Michigan's Upper Peninsula.

My friend Randy Martin had joined a small group of bear hunters, each of whom had their own hounds. The men would follow the hounds, taking turns having their own hounds in the hunt. In this hunt Randy did not have his hounds with him. They were stashed away in pens back at the lodge awaiting their turn to get into a hunt. They had not been in the field very long when they picked up the scent of a bear, and the chase and fight sequence began.

They were bear hunting with the usual six big hounds and nearing the end of a chase. They could tell by the sound of the dogs that there was a big bear fight on the ground. As they neared the fight scene the sound of the hounds changed into the sound of a running fight. Meaning, the dogs had left the fight area and the bear was running again. Almost immediately the baying of the hounds changed again indicating the bear was through running and had climbed and sought refuge in a tree some 30 yards from the fight scene.

When they came upon the fight scene, they could see the body of one of the dogs that had been killed lying on the ground. This was not the usual bear-type killing. The dog's complete body had been stripped naked and the skin was gone.

The hunters thought that the dead dog had probably been wounded and could not keep up with the rest of the chasing dogs and fell prey to a pack of wolves that must have been following the hunt for the bear from a distance. The human-shy wolves must have heard the hunters coming through the brush, grabbed the skin, and left with it, only to return to devour the dog's remains when the hunters had gone. The hunters did not have time to stay with the dead dog. They must get to the treed bear to protect what dogs they had left and put an end to a long chase.

When they had taken the bear they walked back to where the fight had occurred and wondered what to do with the body of the dead dog. Randy had experienced the loss of a hound to the wolves and said the first thing to do was to call the Department of Natural Resources. They are the people responsible for bringing the wolves to Upper Michigan and liked to keep track of the wolf packs and their activities.

The DNR officer met with the men and identified marks on the dead dog as a wolf kill. He told them they are typical predators and the whole pack would concentrate on one victim, and there would be no escape for the prey.

They buried the dog's dead body and called off the rest of the day's hunting.

It is sad to lose or have a dog hurt, but in this case, although Randy did not have a dog in this fight, he felt remorse because the slain dog was young and a part-time bear dog—and wife's full-time pet. What a story to have to take home.

Just being out-of-doors in Michigan's Upper Peninsula during the early fall is worth the long trip from southern Michigan. A lot of people drive there just to enjoy the beautiful brilliant red and yellow trees contrasting with the evergreens along published routes in fall-color tour brochures.

Randy Martin and his wife, Sue, are especially fortunate by being able to take a fall vacation for a full month at this time. They make their lodging accommodations a year in advance, and this all happens just when the black bear hunting season has opened and the Partridge (Pats) and the Woodcock have also opened.

Running one's bear dogs is not something you can do every day. The dogs and the men must take time off to rest up. On the other hand, if Randy feels rested, he can strap on one of Jerry Gertlemen's "Long Gun Holster" that I loaned him, grab his shotgun, his German Shorthair Pointer that also made the trip, and he and Sue can be hunting in less than thirty minutes in the swamp for Woodcock or in the woods for Pats. What a joy.

Randy had one problem during this trip when his grouse-hunting German Shorthair bird dog escaped from his pen and decided to check out the local territory by himself. After two days of seeking, the dog could not be found, and they had to drive home without him. Fortunately, wife Sue had been hunting with Randy, so no big "lost" dog surprise happened.

      Two days later the dog decided to have someone call his home, and Sue made the 400 mile trip back to be rewarded with a big kiss on the cheek from the dog and a perpetual tail wag in the front seat all the way home.

The Bush Plane

The first spring I spent in Michigan I was invited by some of my friends to accompany them on their annual fishing trip into Ontario, Canada. They made reservations at a fly-in lodge named Pine Portage Lodge on Lake Kabinakagami, popularly known as Kaby Lake. The lake is about 200 miles directly north of Sault Ste. Marie, Canada, and the intent was to be in the lodge the middle of May to be all set to fish for Walleye and Northern Pike on opening day of the fishing season.

The plan was to meet and drive from mid-Michigan north to Mackinaw City, some 240 miles, across the huge 5-mile-long Mackinac Bridge whose mid-span is some 250 feet above the water line. The bridge spans the junction of Lake Michigan and Lake Huron, and you can see the long veranda of the world-famous Grand Hotel on Mackinac Island about 4 miles across the open water; then to continue on I-75 north, 52 miles to Sault Ste. Marie, Michigan, and the Canadian border.

Unfortunately, something unusual happens to deer hunters and fishermen when they cross the bridge from Sault Ste. Marie, Michigan, into Sault Ste. Marie, Canada. It is mandatory to stop at the Duty Free Store. People who drink only on Saint Patrick's Day and red state presidential election wins find the lure of a large Canadian quart of their favorite brand of alcoholic headache, sans federal tax, irresistible. They found it quite the macho thing to be seen coming from a liquor store in their killing clothes, with a hunting knife in their belt (on the left side to execute a cross-handed draw if he needed the knife quickly in an emergency), carrying a full liter of booze unadorned, by the neck, and showing the start of a period of no-shave stubble.

Crossing the ship locks between Lake Superior on the left and St. Mary's River that flows into Lake Huron on the right, passing by customs, we were now ready to resume our journey to Wawa, Ontario, 130 miles north on Route 17, where we would get a Bush Plane ride into the wilds of central Canada.

This trip north along the eastern shoreline of Lake Superior and the rugged mountainous terrain past Batchawana and Agawa

Bays is well worth the trip just to enjoy the view.

It is easy to tell when you reach the town of Wawa. It is where the builders of the Canadian Pacific railroad from the West met the builders from the East. There was no Golden Spike driven and then removed there. There is a beautiful 20-foot-high statue of a Canadian Goose.

Motel and dinner were next, and a visit with new friends and fellow veterans at the Canadian Legion Club.

Before I came to Michigan I worked as a Zone Engineer for the Stran Steel Corporation, a Division of National Steel, based in Chicago where I covered fourteen states, mostly by commercial aviation. This was a time when airline companies pampered their passengers with a good free lunch or dinner with soft drinks and coffee, made sure you were buckled in securely, gave you a small pillow, made you aware of what to do if the plane went down in water, and how to exit the plane in case of a ground emergency. If you happened to be on a scheduled flight from Minneapolis to Duluth, Minnesota, on North Central Airlines in the winter on an unheated two-engine DC-3, you were the recipient of an olive drab U. S. Army wool blanket to keep you warm.

My first exposure to a Canadian bush plane was a single-engine DeHavoland Beaver equipped with pontoons. Since it was in mid-May, to take advantage of the opening day of the fishing season, I, at the advice of my veteran Canadian fishing friends, was well prepared for anticipated cold or wet weather, and I had most of the cold weather clothes I owned. I also had most of the fishing tackle I owned.

I was surprised at the amount of baggage my companions were taking, and that included a large freezer to bring their catch home. This freezer also served as a first class seat on the flight into the Canadian wilds.

I was also surprised at the size of the airplane. More surprised that a small pick-up load of fishing gear and clothes were loaded first. I kept looking for the seating arrangements, the seat belt locations, and safety procedures. And I was told, "You have a duffle bag. Sit on it. You do not need a seat belt."

Safety instructions? What if the plane goes down over water? What if the plane goes down over land? If we went down

over land there are trees, and they would break our fall. If we went down over water, we had pontoons and should be all right. If all else fails, and you had to exit the plane and have not figured when by now, the pilot will throw you out the door. This might be a good time to pop the cork on the big jug.

Being overloaded and with no wind, the pilot could not get the plane off the water. He went as far as he could down the lake, turned the plane around, and sped back to the original starting place in such a manner that large waves were created in the water. No problem. The pilot turned the plane around, revved the engine to maximum, headed down the lake, lifted one pontoon off the waves, and bounced the other pontoon off the top of another wave, gained speed, and we were airborne.

We flew some 75 miles over wilderness to the fishing lodge with the intent to land in the lake in front of the lodge. However, the lake was still covered with 6 inches of ice, and landing was not possible.

Fortunately, the lodge was located near the mouth of the river emptying the lake, and it was decided to try and land in the river. The pilot thought it would be fine because the snow had started to melt causing a spring raise, and the river was high.

No problem. Like the pilot said, "Coming down is easy.

Getting up is harder."

The landing was fine, and a truck came to take us to the lodge. We celebrated our safe landing in the warm lodge with some giant 6 inch ice crystals from the lake and tax-free liquid from the USA. It was another ho-hum trip for everybody but me.

Just one problem: We still had to fly out. And assuming we did not get fogged in, which happens occasionally, a week's stay in camp might turn into three extra days of unplanned fishing.

The next morning was a bright and sunny day, and we were all dressed in our winter clothes prepared to fish through the ice someway. The guides broke through the 300 yards of 6 inch ice to open water, and we were on our way.

This was my experience of fishing with a hired guide. The guides were all Canadians, and some were Indians. They all knew every corner of the lake and were in competition with other guides with the size and quantity of fish.

My previous experience with fishing had to do with manhandling an outboard motor, hoping it would start when you finally got it situated on the boat's transom board. Then carrying all your fishing tackle, dip net, oars, extra clothes, etc., and putting all it out of the way somehow. And when you finally got underway, you try and guess where you fished last time, bay or river. Then it was how deep to fish and what kind of bait to use, and a lot of other things, including the things you left in the car or at home.

At Pine Portage Lodge, after you had a big breakfast served, you went back to the cabin and got your fishing clothes on and all your rods, tackle box, etc. The guide would meet you at your boat, take your gear, see that you were seated properly to his specifications, show you where the life preserves were located, and leave promptly at eight o'clock.

The whole area was travelogue perfect. The sun was up when we left the lodge, and with a brilliant blue sky and the sparkling white wake streaming out behind the racing boat atop looking-glass-smooth, deep blue water that contrasted with the bright green trees that came down to the water's edge, it was a pleasure to be a guest in this wonderland.

This was indeed a wilderness. There were no roads into the lake. Supplies had to be brought to the lake in small boats, except in the winter when the lake is frozen over and trucks could drive on the ice.

There was another lodge at the south end of the lake, but we never had to go that far, some 15 miles, to catch the fish we needed. There was an old one-trapper, one-room cabin about 12 feet square with no door and a roof about half gone. We went in this cabin one time to get out of the rain, but with the heavy snow accumulation it didn't have many years to last, and we watched it deteriorate over time.

There was a year-round house on the far west side of the lake where a stream came into the lake. This house had been recently vacated. It was referred to as "Old Kate's" house. It seems her husband had died, and she grew old and could not take care of herself year round, so the authorities came and took her to live in the closest town. The authorities came back and shot her dogs to keep them from running wild in a pack, and they left vacant a furnished home.

One of the other things I had never seen was a gigantic eagle's nest high up in one of the big trees. It looked like it could be 7 or 8 feet in diameter and was located on the west side of the lake near Fairy Creek.

Fairy Creek was quite a place. The creek was not wide enough because of the bushy sides for a boat to penetrate, but it was an ideal place for River Carp to spawn. Spawning Carp mean one thing: dinner bell for large Northern Pike.

The pike we caught there were 20 to 30 pounds and about 35 to 45 inches long (fisherman's prerogative: weight and length approximate). The crystal clear water about 50 feet from the creek's mouth was only about 3 feet deep, and when one of the big fish, no longer hungry and not interested in any of our bait, swam slowly by our boat, and you leaned over the side to see it, being that close to one's eyes made it seem like it was 6 feet long.

The last thing I remember hearing about Fairy Creek was much later, when a man I know came into some unexpected money and perpetuated the "Ugly American" name when he, fishing by himself, showed up at the lodge with a large stringer of very large Northern Pike.

It seemed he came into Canada and applied and received a permit to take a Black Bear. He also brought into Canada, illegally, a high-powered hand gun. He took his boat close to the mouth of

117

Fairy creek, and when one of the big fish came close to the boat, he would shoot the gun into the water near or at the fish. This would stun the fish enough for them to remain motionless long enough for him to retrieve the fish by hand or by dip net.

He also decided he did not want to go into the woods and wait near a bait pile until a bear came along. So he told one of the guides he would give him his new high-powered rifle if he would bag a bear for him.

The guide agreed and within a matter of few minutes a shot was heard from behind the lodge. The guide had walked back some 100 yards to the garbage dump behind the kitchen and shot a semi-tame camp bear.

The last time I heard of this game violator, he had spent more of someone else's money than he was entitled to and was spending some time in the state prison.

But now back to some more pleasant things.

After a short twenty to thirty minute comfortable boat ride, with the guide facing into the wind and you snug with a hood on your coat, the guide would get you to the place that would be the most productive fishing for 2 to 3 pound Walleyes and maybe a big Northern.

One of the most exciting things that happened that first day was when my brother George, who was my fishing buddy that day, hooked into a big fish.

We were fishing in a little bay that would have been a grassy meadow before the spring water runoff flooded it. We knew it was a big fish because we had two big men fishing, and a guide in an aluminum boat and motor, and the fish was towing us around the little lake. George was using a light test line, and he had to let the fish run out of steam before he could get him close enough for the huge dip net

There was another boat with our friends fishing in the same bay, and they stopped to watch, anxiously waiting to get a glimpse of the big fish. When George got the fish close enough, he was the first to identify the fish, and he immediately started to laugh.

He had traveled over a thousand miles by plane and car to catch a huge 15-pound river carp that did not bite the bait, but got in the way of George's line and was hooked in the dorsal fin on its back. This is the same type of fish that he had caught hundreds, maybe thousands of times, when he was a young man and he and my father were commercial fishermen on the Missouri River, literally ten minutes from his home.

George released the fish so he could be active in the ongoing spawning run. This had to be the luckiest carp in the world. If he had been caught elsewhere in the United States he stood a good chance of getting into someone's cornmeal bowl and dipped piecemeal into hot grease. Or like my good friend, Tony Watson, described about having sushi dinner with the president of a corporation in Tokyo to whom Tony was selling large machinery. The waiter brought a large carp intact on a platter. The fish filets were in place on the plate, and the whole filet was cut into one-inch square pieces to be picked up individually and eaten. Tony lost his appetite when the fish lifted up his tail and displaced a couple pieces. The fish was still alive! I guess when you order fresh fish in Japan that is what you get. What a contrast: Sushi in Tokyo and shore lunch in the Canadian wilderness.

We always caught a lot of fish on Kaby Lake, and about

halfway through the morning the guide started separating just the right size Walleyes, which we found out later were to be our shore lunch.

There were several lunch sites. A lunch site means there is enough dry area for two or three boats to land, enough room for a half dozen men to sit or lay on the ground, and enough room to build a cooking fire.

Each boat had a guide, and they shared the work of cleaning the fish, building a fire, and preparing any of the other food brought from the camp like condiments, coffee, and fresh homemade bread.

Fishing was good, and the highlight of the meal was the freshly caught Walleye filets fried to a golden brown and eaten with your fingers. Fresh homemade bread made the shore lunch a complete success.

The weather made an abrupt change and warmed up so much that everybody was soon fishing in their t-shirts, and when we motored back to the lodge at the end of the day, the ice had crumbled and melted, and completely floated away. After being out on the water all day we were all ready to head back to the lodge. We were glad to see five o'clock arrive.

This was my first exposure to professional guides, and when they do these things for you, it could almost become a necessary thing on my next fishing trip anywhere.

The guides take you to where the fish are. They bait your hook, take a fish off your line, re-bait your line if you are losing bait or replace a plug or fly if that is what you are using, put the fish on a stringer for keeping, and get your lure loose when you get it caught in a tree or a snag in the water. If you cannot catch a fish he will use his pole to help, especially if you do not have enough fish for lunch, use the dip net to land your fish, a fishing technique advisor, open your can of beer (join you in a beer if you have any left on the way to the lodge), clean, wrap, and freeze your catch to take home with you…and they are all-around good fellows.

It seemed like a very short ride back to the lodge, and it was time again for the long ice crystals and alcoholic libation while the guides cleaned the fish.

Dinner at the lodge was an hour later, and I do not remember any outstanding food we had, but I know that after being on the water all day no food was ever rejected and everyone ate too much. I do remember the house specialty was the fresh caught fish in chowder that matched or beat any New England clam chowder I have ever had.

Then it was back to the cabin and a short-lived nickel-dime poker game with the several young people participating, and then all too early to bed, looking forward for that one big fish just waiting to be caught tomorrow.

For some ten years I went fishing in Canada, and we always stayed at Dick Watson's Pine Portage Lodge. The fishing season always opened in mid-May which coincided with my wedding anniversary, and an understanding wife celebrated by herself with the promise we would take a trip somewhere on the upcoming Memorial Day.

The main lodge building consisted of a dining room, a kitchen, and a small store. The store was stocked with miscellaneous fishing necessities because all of the things that you used successfully back home would not work in this lake. But they were overstocked with the hottest lures that would catch big fish in this lake, and after coming all this way you had to have them.

There were several separate cabins up a slight hill overlooking the bay in front of the lodge in which we stayed. The cabins had room for eight men and had tables, chairs, modern bathrooms, and wood burning stoves.

One year we had built a fire in the stove and stocked the wood pile with "gopher wood" white birch. It was called that because it burned so fast you must "go fer another log." During the night we apparently put too much wood in the stove when we stoked the fire to last all night, and some of the stacked wood fell against the hot stove. We all slept very soundly until the room, now filled with deadly smoke, woke somebody up, who then woke the rest of us. No one was injured. We had just a couple of sore throats from the smoke in the morning.

We were always some of the first people there to take advantage of the May 15th opening day fishing. Another advantage was being there before the black flies had hatched. Consequently, the opening day could require heavy clothes for cold weather, and the gentler sex was rarely seen.

Thinking of this and the cabin reminds me of a good friend that I played golf with occasionally. At that time I did not know he was a regular visitor to the lodge later in the year after the swarming, biting black flies were not so active. This is a story my good friend, Tony, enjoyed telling about himself when he brought friends and relatives with him in the later season.

During that time a lot of women accompanied their husbands and enjoyed the fishing as much as the men. Not all of them showed up for breakfast, but they were all present for dinner and stayed in the dining room afterwards enjoying the fishing stories and whatever beer or cocktails with their husbands.

It was customary for everyone to bring at least one case of beer, as well as the big liter bottles of your favorite headache-producer. This is the only time I participated in taking at least a six-pack of beer in the boat with me, and everyone started drinking by mid-morning. We did share the beer with the local guide if we had any left at the end of the day, if he was not an Indian. (I was involved in teaching a course in the United States Power Squadron at that time. It is an organization dedicated to the teaching of water safety, and they frown on drinking when you are the skipper of a boat. My taking along a six-pack while fishing from a boat is not a thing I would like the students to know about.)

Now back to Tony. The first night in camp everyone was worn out from being on the water at eight o'clock in the morning until five in the afternoon. This calls for a token libation, more or less, in the cabins before dinner, then dinner and early to bed. However, the next night everyone stayed after dinner to meet new friends and get caught up on the day's activities, like the big fish that got away, visiting Old Kate's house, or the huge Bald Eagle's nest near Fairy Creek.

The second night, Tony stayed in the dining room enjoying his new friends and their ladies, and since he was not accustomed to over-indulging in the pursuit of hops-based, brown colored liquids, he found a certain need to visit the restroom that was continually backed up by a line of women and men waiting their turn.

He could wait no longer. The next available place was up the hill in his one of six look-alike cabins. He knew at least two of his fishing companions had long since gone to bed, and since they were a little bit nervous walking to the cabin in the dark because they had seen wild black bears not too far from the lodge earlier in the day, he thought he would enliven the evening for them.

He was surprised the door to the cabin was locked, and immediately started growling like a bear and scratching on the door with his fingernails, hoping they thought there was a bear at the door. But he could wait no longer to get to the inside restroom and started relieving himself on the door.

He heard the door being unlocked, and the door was opened a crack. A flashlight was shone out the door. He heard a woman's voice say, "Honey, what is it?" And a man replying, "I don't know, just somebody growling like a bear, scratching on the door, and relieving himself on the front porch while wearing a bright yellow windbreaker." Oops, wrong cabin.

At this point Tony thought it was better to be among the missing, and he walked slowly away. He was wondering how he could face the breakfast people in the morning when by now everybody would be in attendance. The story would surely be passed around, and everybody would be looking for his bright yellow jacket.

Since the weather was very cool in the mornings, and Tony had only one jacket, he thought he had a problem. At this point, he recalled the Boy Scout motto (or whatever they call them in England, his native land), "Be prepared."

His new, yellow windbreaker was reversible, and it was totally black inside. I am sure at breakfast time he had an unspoken "not me" expression on his face as he hurriedly downed his food and headed for the waiting guide in his boat.

So that's my story about Kaby Lake and fishing in Canada. I enjoyed that first trip and the good times I shared with my companions, in spite of cold weather, fishing in the rain, and knowing you would be wearing your rain suits all day and not even think about going back to the lodge.

The great numbers of fish caught kept you wondering about

what happened that day as you rode back to the lodge. The days passed so fast. But best of all was the great, fresh, golden-brown Walleye shore lunch. I did not believe we could eat so much fish.

I am going back in spite of the plane ride, and the weather, and the afternoons when you couldn't catch a keeper fish.

Maybe next year.

The author in Canada

Buck'n Bear Club

A friend phoned me to set up a meeting in Mt Pleasant, Michigan, with the intent to visit some vacant land in Northern Lower Michigan, not far from the famous Mackinaw Bridge.

One of the men at the meeting had a good friend named Charley Schaar. He was a school teacher and part-time deer and bear hunter who lived in the small town of Onaway, Michigan.

Charley had informed my friend that there was a large parcel of land up for lease in wild, undeveloped woods and swamp located north of Rogers City and bordering on Lake Huron on the east side. This land was just east of Black Lake and Black Mountain, Michigan.

The land was owned by the Abitibi Lumber Company and consisted of some thirty thousand acres. This timber land was being clear-cut, primarily in the winter when the lowland or swamp was frozen and allowed the heavy tree cutting machines to operate in safety.

It was portioned off and leased to groups of men who would use the land for the formation of hunting clubs. There were to be twenty-three separate parcels to lease, and the cost of the lease would be equal to the yearly property taxes.

My friend in Mt. Pleasant had a plat of the property, and after a short discussion it was determined to visit the site, in particular, Parcel #23, as soon as possible. Parcel 23 was one of the last areas available and consisted of 1,300 acres of woods and swamp.

Not long after, on a beautiful, late spring day, we motored our way north on I-75 through Gaylord, Michigan. Driving down the long hills it was a pleasure to see the multi-colored trees in the fall, but this particular road was very treacherous if the first big snowfall came just before deer hunting season opened when traffic is almost bumper to bumper.

We exited I-75 at Indian River, headed east to Onaway to pick up Charley, and then headed north around Black Lake. We finally came out of the hills and drove a short way to the east on Route 68 toward Lake Huron. It was a drop in elevation of some 680 feet from Gaylord.

The entrance was about 3 miles west of Lake Huron and was heavily wooded on both sides with huge maple trees bending over the sand-covered road and leaves touching in the center of the road.

This short drive was a joy to experience in the fall when all the leaves turned a magnificent bright yellow with a brilliant sunlight reflecting downward off each leaf. It seemed like an old master's painting when you drove through the tunnel of light. The trees certainly contributed their part to the famous Northern Michigan color tours.

We headed north on the sand-covered logging road that wound through dense woods for about a half a mile, until we came to an east-to-west logging road that was the southern property line of Parcel 23.

Our friend Charley, who had hunted in this area before it was bought by Abitibi Lumber, gave us a complete tour of the land to see if we were interested, but I had made up my mind to go for the lease five minutes after we entered the property. The land was heavily wooded with birch, cedar and various hardwood trees. There were clear-cut areas about 100 yards wide running east and west that were cut sometime in the previous ten years and separated by uncut wooded areas about 400 yards wide.

This layout of cutting made for an excellent location of deer hunting blinds. There were many signs of a good deer population. Markings on the ground and scrapes on the saplings showed signs of activity in the previous fall.

When we walked off the logging roads we jumped partridge that were scattered around, and we were told that the area was a good stopping place for woodcock in their migratory flight in the fall.

There were swampy areas with drainage ditches to facilitate spring snowmelt and rain runoff. These ditches were mainly enlarged natural drain areas and moved the water from west to east into Lake Huron.

Abitibi ceased their logging during the whitetail deer hunting season, because with twenty-three hunt clubs averaging fifteen members each, it would mean over three hundred high-powered weapons firing a missile that would carry over a mile sometime during the day.

After the tour, the site for the future cabin selected itself on a wooded ridge right next to one of the logging roads. The site was a few feet higher than the swamp areas to the east, and to the west were open woods with very little groundcover. The cabin was to face south down the logging road.

We all agreed to go with the lease, but now the inevitable problems presented themselves. But by the time we got to Mt. Pleasant we had most of them solved, like who could we get as members, how would we get them, how much would it cost each, and what kind of building could we build.

The proposed lease was very lenient and pertained mostly to good housekeeping chores, insurance coverage, and a stipulation that if you had a house trailer for a cabin it must have wheels in place for easy removal. No permanent structures were to be built, and a security deposit was to be used if the leaser had to remove the structure.

The lease cost, which was the amount of the property taxes, only totaled $1,755, with the stipulation of an anticipated tax increase of 10% per year. With a membership of twenty men and even a nominal charge of $400, it would make the construction of a building viable.

When we got back to Mt. Pleasant it was decided to set up a meeting at the Embers Restaurant and invite a lot of our friends who were mostly in the construction business.

When a man works outside all day and comes in at night hungry, the thought of the famous Embers Restaurant's one-pound barbeque pork chop is too hard to resist. We soon had everyone in an agreeable state of mind, and the establishment of our own private hunting club had the necessary twenty members we needed for the project to proceed.

Then, after a long discussion, we voted to call the club the "Buck'n Bear Hunting Club." We asked one of our members who happened to be a charactorist, to design a logo showing a buck, a bear, and a hunter. This was soon done and accepted after a certain masculine protuberance was replaced by a whisky bottle, and we had our logo.

All of these men were hunters, and most of them had their own property, hunted on a friend's property, or hunted on public lands. But the thought of belonging to a hunting club in Northern Lower Michigan for only a few hundred dollars a year was irresistible.

We had a vast assortment of people in our membership. A lot of these people were involved in general contracting and were versed in all forms of labor that we needed. We had a metal building contractor, a concrete contractor, a master plumber, carpenters, and steel workers. There was an electrician, an IBM employee, a radio station manager, an insurance man, a musician in a guitar band, and we even had an ex-hippy charactorist who traveled all over the Midwest trading his artwork for gasoline for his old car when cash ran short. He became his own charactorist when he later moved to the Keys of Florida, lived on his own big sailboat, and became a finish carpenter for a living. He grew a huge white beard, and one year he won the yearly-held Ernest Hemmingway look-alike contest.

Since we could get a sizeable discount on the cost of a metal building, it was decided to proceed in that direction. The lease said no permanent structures, and Abitibi Lumber could see the building was certainly a temporary structure because it was bolted and screwed together, and the whole building could be taken down

128

piece by piece and easily be removed. They never questioned the concrete floor. (Since selling metal buildings was my livelihood, I could rationalize that when I talked to potential customers I could claim my metal building would stand for a hundred years if the interior is protected from the weather and that I would personally guarantee it for fifty years. That timeframe surpassed normal longevity by about twenty-five years, so I felt pretty safe making that statement, and most people saw the humor therein.)

We signed the lease, and with a nominal cost we were in business. It was too late to get the building planned that same year, but some of our members hunted on the property in the fall and stayed in campers on the back of their pickups.

We decided if we made the building 24 feet wide and 32 feet long and 16 feet high, we would have room for a second floor for sleeping purposes. We poured the concrete floor and erected the steel building the following spring.

A couple of the carpenters went into the woods, cut down a solid tree, and made columns to support the second deck. They then went to the local lumber yard and bought plywood for the second deck and enough lumber for rafters and perimeter 2x4s to support the deck. They also built wooden stairs to the upper deck. They did all of this without any plans or drawings. They just knew what to do, and they did it all in one weekend.

Our first thought, since the cabin was in a very isolated area, was that it would be better if we had minimum windows to protect the material inside. However, it seemed to be too dark in the day, and one of the men brought and put in a picture window on the west side of the building looking into the nearly clear area among some big trees. He also put a window in the upper deck looking down the southern entry to our lease. It was nice to have this kind of talent in-house.

It was not long before we got rid of our Coleman lanterns and installed propane gas lines for our new (used) cook stove and ceiling lights. Someone owned a log splitter, and we cut enough firewood in a September work-weekend for our giant pot-bellied furnace, which was replaced by a new stove from one our contractor's remodeling jobs. Our dining table was a masterpiece. One of our guys brought a 12-to-14 foot long piece of a bowling alley lane that was 4 inches wide, about 3 inches thick, and had a hard maple, indestructible finish. Our membership fluctuated, and finally dropped to fourteen to fifteen members, and the table made in the shape of a picnic table was nearly long enough to seat most of our people at meal time.

The whole structure was a typical maintenance-free steel building, and we had no problems until someone decided to break into the building the hard way. Thankfully they did not just break the big picture window. They decided to get on top of the roof, tear off one of the screwed-down 3x17 foot metal panels. What they did not count on was the panels being of extremely hard, high tensile strength. They finally ripped a panel half way across, just enough for a man to slip into the upper deck.

Nothing much was taken except a few things a person would need to stock his own hunting club. One of the things we really missed was our huge 18-inch skillet. We had great food out of this skillet, such as fresh deer meat, fried potatoes with onions, and even beef stroganoff.

This was a great place to be outside in the fall. Some of us who were bird shooters especially enjoyed hunting the grouse, and enjoyed the cooked birds even more. There were migrating woodcock to be had if the weather was not bad enough to hurry them on their way south. We put up a buck pole our first year and got a few deer every year, but most of us were not too concerned about bagging a dear every year.

On opening day of deer season most of the members showed up, but after the third day most of them went someplace else to do their hunting. Then it was the most enjoyable time. It was up before daylight and into the deer blinds waiting for the deer that rarely came by. About eight o'clock, especially if it was cold outside, it was going back to the cabin for hot coffee and doughnut, and maybe a nice nap until noon when everyone would start coming in for lunch.

Late afternoon was the same procedure, and someone was always back early to start up the fire in the furnace and get supper under way. If someone had been lucky with bagging a deer, usually deer tenderloin or liver or chops would be forthcoming. If the deer had been bagged a couple of days prior we might have a deer heart marinating, and it was our supper.

When opening day comes most hunters are burdened with a variety of things they must have to take to the blind to compete with the wary deer. He would have heavy boots, hunting pants, wool shirt, vest, light coat, colored hunting coat, and hat and sunglasses. He would also be wearing a hunting knife that is constantly being honed when sitting in the cabin. He would have a heavy deer rifle and a box of twenty cartridges somewhere on his person, either in the rifle or his pocket. He must also have a lunch sack, a thermos of coffee, and a compass on a string looped around his neck. Most of all he would have a flashlight to find his way back through the woods after dark, hoping he could pick up the fluorescent blazes on the trees leading back to the cabin. He may also have a handheld whistle decoy to imitate a deer noise and perhaps two antlers to hit together making like two bucks are dueling over a doe.

By the third day though most of the material mentioned above is left by the hunter in the cabin, except maybe for a couple of shells in his shirt pocket and a thermos of coffee.

This is no hit-or-miss operation. He would be in the blind before daylight and until after dark. No lunch break in the cabin. He stayed solid in the blind. And in one case, he would not panic after hearing a noise behind him, even when he rose up to look and saw a full-grown black bear rise up out of the weeds on his hind legs at the same time, and look him right in the eye from 50 yards away. Fortunately, the bear left the area first. What a great tale for telling in the cabin and future generations.

I have only seen one black bear when hunting, and it was a very enjoyable event. Earlier in the day when walking down a road to my blind, I had seen small tracks in the snow of a bear that crossed the road. I was surprised that there was no sign of tracks belonging to the mother bear.

Later in the day I had moved into a glade in the swamp and was sitting on a falling log waiting for a deer that someone had spooked to come passing by. My rifle was at the end of my reach, but it was close enough if I spotted a deer as it came sneaking through the swamp as there a lot of hunters in the woods keeping the deer moving. Then, as if by magic, this beautiful little bear was walking right toward me. He had to have been born the previous spring, and I would say he was about half grown.

His coat was a very shiny black, and he looked like a giant teddy bear as he kept coming toward me. I was not afraid of him, and felt I was sort of safe since I did not see his mother's tracks earlier in the morning. When he was about 30 feet away I gave out a low whistle, and he was out of sight in an instant. It was a lifelong memory for me, and I hope it reinforced his fear of humans.

Deer hunting can be very exciting, especially one's first deer. Once a deer has been stalked and killed, the excitement fades and reality sinks in, and the real work begins. If your successful hunt happens in broad daylight, you can usually follow the deer's exit path if the kill was not instant and the deer sped out of sight. The deer will probably head into heavy cover to hide and will soon be found dead. However, some deer cannot be found the same day, and a longer hunt will be required. This is more likely to happen when a deer is shot late in the afternoon.

Once the dead animal is found, the first chore is the field stripping. This will reduce the weight of the animal by about twenty-five to thirty percent, which means the deer will still weight near one hundred pounds. This is a lot of weight to carry out of a swamp or through downed trees and brush by oneself. Once the deer is hung by the horns on the buck pole, one finally realizes a lot of work remains, and this you do by yourself.

The deer must then be put in your car for the drive home, with a stop to register the deer with the Department of Natural Resources, and then try to find a butcher who is probably open just during deer season to handle the deer.

You turn the deer over to the butcher, describing how you want the meat handled with a quantity of the butcher's special recipe for buckburger or seasoned sausage, etc. All your food is packaged and frozen, and ready for your home freezer. The venison is delicious when prepared at home, and yet when the next fall comes and you make sure you have enough room in your freezer for your new buck, you find most of last year's venison is still frozen and must be discarded.

Also, at this time you save the trophy hide to fashion into some kind of doeskin wear. Your deer skin must be taken to be tanned. And there are the antlers. If the antlers are large and you would like to have them to be displayed in your home, they must be saved. Or, if it is a real large rack, a trip to the taxidermist for a head and shoulder mount can be made. Having a trophy set of antlers is more like having a pet that you have to take care of for the rest of your life. They do not need much maintenance but they seem to be in your life forever, and are finally given away or just discarded.

Needless to say, it is a lot easier to sit and enjoy the successful efforts of other hunters, and celebrate with them until they load the trophy buck into the back of their car and are on their way home for the conclusion of the hunt by themselves.

From time to time our club membership dwindled, and we were always on the lookout for new members. I talked my good friend Jay Rogers from Traverse City into joining, and he became an important member. He was the one who cut and installed a picture window in one of our metal walls.

Jay decided he would like to moose hunt, and he hired a Canadian outfitter to fly him into a lake that was located north of a certain base line to fill his moose license. He made a long drive into Canada, boarded a bush plane, and was dropped off at a lake where he was assured there were plenty of moose around.

He scouted around for a couple of days, found a lot of moose signs, and felt he was ready to hunt seriously. He was out of camp early, and while he was hunting in very rough woods he could hear a moose very close to him, but between the two of them—man and moose—was a grove of very close-together saplings and heavy groundcover.

The hunter felt the only way he could get to the moose was to crawl on the ground. The ground however was covered with a lot of dried leaves, and it was going to be impossible the get where he wanted to go without making a lot of noise, and the moose would probably take off for parts unknown.

He made an excellent stalk, and when he got to where he thought the moose would be, he lifted up his head to look, and found the moose had not moved and was very close, staring right at Jay. At this point it was hard to tell who is the hunter and who is the huntee. Being that close to a very large male animal during the rutting season is not a totally safe place to be.

After the hunter decided to shoot his rifle, he had trouble finding just where the safety lever was located. He was leaning back, almost sitting on his heels and shooting from the hip. Once he had the safety off, he fired his rifle. One shot, one moose down, one successful hunt.

Jay was a general contractor and a builder of very expensive homes, and he could envision the big rack (and of course it had to be a full head and shoulder mount) in that special place over the fireplace in the unfinished lower level of his own self-built home. This would also give him an excuse to totally finish the room, and quiet the periodic wifely reminders of same.

The best of all would be the large amount of meat. The moose was much bigger than a cow, and the amount of roasts, filets, etc., had to be mouthwatering to someone who had just been in the woods long enough to enjoy this kind of home cooking.

Now all they had to do was call for the outfitter to send the plane to pick up the hunter and his moose. No problem. The plane landed back at the outfitter's lake, and when the pilot taxied to the dock they were met by a bunch of people congratulating him on taking the huge moose.

One of the smiling faces in the crowd announced himself as a game warden. He said they liked to keep track of the bigger moose taken, and then asked the pilot where they got the moose. The pilot was very confident about where they had been, and he named the lake and a brief description it. The warden asked the pilot if he was sure of the lake, and the pilot said he was.

The warden unfolded his chart and said that the lake was above a certain base line and that was a no-hunting area. He would have to confiscate the moose, and said there would be monetary penalties to the hunter for shooting it—and that the hunter was under arrest! He was allowed, much later, to go home, but the moose stayed. There would be a court trial, and it might be a good time to get a lawyer.

Jay wanted his moose and his money back from the outfitter who claimed it was not his fault. He also thought the flying service that provided the plane and pilot ought to pay the fines.

All I remember is that there was a court appearance and Jay was cleared, got his money back from the outfitter, and after a year and a half his moose was released to him. I do know there was good food in the freezer for a long time.

Now that he had his trophy moose back, it was time to visit the taxidermy shop and have a rack and full shoulder mount made. He later picked up the mount in his pickup, and then the big, long-awaited day came. The head was going to its rightful place above the fireplace in the lower level, and the whole family was there to watch the event.

One fatal problem occurred. There was no way the head could fit in the narrow confines of a standard width stairway. The moose could not stay in the house, but the hunter had his office in the front of a metal building, and his shop area was behind the office. It was finally decided the shop area had to be the new home for the giant mount.

I used to visit Jay periodically, and often checked the status of the big moose. He finally sold his business, and I would bet the moose made the move with the hunter. After all, as I said, if you get a trophy, he is yours for life.

But now back to the Buck'n Bear. After everyone had been in camp for a few days, they fell into a routine: get up early, into the blind before daylight, and by ten o'clock all were completely bored because the deer had a routine too. There were no more deer running around in broad daylight.

This routine worked for everyone except Charlie, who at times seemed to attract deer that were looking for him. His routine was the same as everyone else's routine, except he would hunt early, then drive the ten miles to the high school and be there in time to teach his morning classes. He did take time to leave his blaze-orange hunting coat, hat, pants, and boots in the cabin so he could suit up in time for an evening hunt…if he did not have basketball practice that night.

Big mistake. One morning he bagged a dear early at first legal light. He hurriedly field dressed the deer, took it back to the buck pole in front of the cabin, hung the buck head high, changed into his teaching clothes, and was off to school.

All day he kept thinking how he could proudly drive back to town with the big buck and begin showing it to all his envious teachers. What a combination: full-time teacher, part-time great deer slayer.

When Charley drove to the cabin later that afternoon he looked at the buck pole for his deer, and his first thought was that the white-hooded people had been at work there. The once-proud deer was now wearing Charley's blaze-orange hunting cap and coat, buttoned in place. He also had donned Charley's hunting trousers.

The deer not only had all of Charley's hunting clothes on, but it picked up two other of Charley's human habits. The deer was holding a can of beer, and there was a cigarette in his mouth. This deer had the distinction of being the only one who had been field dressed, dressed, and then had to be undressed to get a ride back to town.

During this particular time, my job took me on the road and away from home about three or four days a week, so I was content to get in camp to just relax and stay there. Most of the other hunters were anxious to get out and see what was happening in the little towns around our camp.

The lure of the great hamburgers and draft beer at the 211 Bar, some five miles away just south of Black Lake, was for some irresistible, and it was the early evening stop. It was the watering hole for other hunters from the hunt clubs, so you could get an idea of how the good the hunting was elsewhere.

The next stop for some would be the local bars in the town of Onaway about five miles south. But for some people, one of the few nights a year they are out alone, the final place would be the Black Bar Inn on Route 23, north of Rogers City, where they had a raised dance floor and imported some amateur dancers from Detroit who tried to imitate strippers from the big bars there.

This was a very congenial crowd, and everybody seemed to be having a great time with the young girls singing and dancing.

Since almost everybody needed a shave, wore their hunting clothes, and still had their hunting knife on their belt, everybody was in a strictly non-violent mood.

Throughout this book there are stories of wild bears and their persecution, but as always with animals, they can sometimes turn the tables on us and get a little bit even.

My good friend, Charley Schaar, was hunting bear in the swamp when his dogs barked treed on a young bear they were chasing. When Charley came up to the tree he could see the bear not very far up in it, and for fear of a young dog being hurt, he proceeded to grab the dog that was getting out of control in an effort to calm her down.

It seems the young bear was as nervous as the dog, and when Charley held the dog and looked up at the bear, he was greeted with a loud blast and a bombastic eruption…and a flood of foul smelling excrement fell and completely covered him and the dog!

This was no time for shyness. He had to remove most of his clothes, grab the dog, and head for the nearest creek. What happened to the bear? No one knows. He got away, and no doubt learned a new method of self-preservation. It was a good win for the bear.

Another charter member of our club was Roger Card. He became a very successful big game hunter, and at one time he had successfully bagged over two hundred animals from all over the world. He has worked with Ferris State College in Big Rapids, Michigan, to establish the "Card Wildlife Education Center," and they have two hundred of his heads on display there.

I mentioned above about Jay Rogers shooting a moose up in Canada. After he left the court house, all he had to do was get in his car and drive home. But on his first of many trips to Africa big game hunting, he spent two or three days on safari just getting to know the country and looking at wildlife before the serious hunting began.

Unfortunately, at that time, the government of Kenya decided to crack down on all the big game poaching going on there and closed the whole country to big game hunting, including licensed safari outfitters. They also thought it would be a good idea if all the safari hunters would leave the country. That was quite a trip for three days of sightseeing, though Roger did manage to hunt there at a later date. Going home was not as easy as Jay's leaving Canada, but both Jay and Roger had the same results. Both came home without the animals they sought.

I talked to Roger recently, and he told me he had taken all of North America's twenty-nine Trophy Animals and thirty-six total species. In January 2006 he received the Safari International World Hunting award.

I moved to East Lansing in the spring, and by the fall I was taken with the idea of having a Big Ten college in my back yard, and I became a Michigan State sports fan. The main trouble I had with my season football tickets was that usually a big game with Michigan or Ohio State would fall on the opening day of the deer season, and I had to be deer hunting.

The other bad thing about the college football season was that our seats were up high, and if the school had a mediocre team I could look over at the trees and see I had just missed another beautiful fall day at the cabin in the woods, or a golf game at one of my favorite courses. Finally, the season tickets had to go.

The entire acreage of the Abitibi property was sold to one developer in the late 1990s, and they let us keep our lease as it was for a short time. They then offered us first opportunity to buy the property of our lease for $1,000 an acre. At that time we were leasing 850 acres, and since all of the members were of nominal means, the purchase was far beyond our capabilities. We found out later that someone had purchased the building and 40 acres around it, and we all just walked away.

I belonged to this club for many years. It has always been my policy, taught to me by my father and a myriad of outdoor literary heroes, that you do not shoot anything you won't eat. Then one day I was shocked to hear the Michigan Department of Natural Resources announced that in their routine testing of slain deer they found that in Presque Isle County, our county in Northern Lower Michigan, some deer were infected with a form of Mad Cow disease and should not be eaten.

So that was the end of the Buck'n Bear Club for me.

North American 29

MINIMUM REQUIREMENTS AND ELIGIBLE CATEGORIES Must have been taken in currently recognized North American habitat. Free range only. Minimum 29 of which 3 sheep are required. Bow minimum 15 of which 2 sheep, 2 bears, 1 moose, 1 elk and 1 caribou are required.

	Score or photo
☐ Jaguar*	_____
☐ Cougar (or puma, or mtn. lion)	_____
☐ Alaskan brown bear	_____
☐ Grizzly bear (common or b.g.)	_____
☐ Polar bear	_____
☐ Inland black bear	_____
☐ Coastal black bear	_____
☐ Gray wolf	_____
☐ American bison (may be estate)	_____
☐ Muskox (b.g. or greenland)	_____
☐ American mountain goat	_____
☐ Dall sheep	_____

	Score or photo
☐ Stone sheep	_____
☐ Rky Mtn or CA bighorn sheep	_____
☐ Desert bighorn sheep	_____
☐ Pronghorn	_____
☐ Rocky Mountain elk	_____
☐ Roosevelt elk	_____
☐ Tule elk	_____
☐ Alaska-Yukon moose	_____
☐ Western Canada moose	_____
☐ Eastern Canada moose	_____
☐ Shiras moose	_____
☐ Alaska-Yukon b.g. caribou	_____

	Score or photo
☐ Central Canada b.g. caribou	_____
☐ Arctic Islands caribou	_____
☐ Mountain caribou	_____
☐ Quebec-Labrador caribou	_____
☐ Woodland caribou	_____
☐ Rocky Mountain mule deer	_____
☐ Desert mule deer	_____
☐ Columbia black-tailed deer	_____
☐ Sitka black-tailed deer	_____
☐ White-tailed deer	_____
☐ Coues white-tailed deer	_____
☐ American alligator	_____

*Darted or Record Book entry before 1972
The jaguar is not required but can be substituted for another category.

Closing Thoughts

World War II ended the childhood Lickskillet I knew.

The boys I played with either went to war or just plain moved away. Steve Gabick, Charles Sanders, Billy Bob Hart, Carl Baker, Walter Metz, Morrel Lurry, Art Barthel, Jimmy Rhyne, John O'Harron, and Chris Holthusen had all left.

Most went into the service as volunteers and grew into manhood overnight. Some were wounded in the service; one that I know of was killed onboard a naval vessel during an air raid in Naples, Italy. Most came home for a brief visit, and then left for good.

This might be the last of my Lickskillet writing. On the other hand, I still have half of the old scrapbook to be delved into, and there are over one hundred years of the Leavenworth Times easily accessible on file.

There should be someone to write the unique activities of the old shipyard and the fabricating plant while the sons and daughters of the work force are still alive.

There is a wealth of information and pictures available, and I have found that people are willing to talk to you, loan you pictures and even donate pictures to the library or the museum if only their name as a donor was mentioned.

I may be the one to write it someday, but for now? Goodbye old Lickskillet.

Author Notes

The cover art was created by former Leavenworth resident artist, Gary Montgomery, the brother of author Wolf Montgomery. The scene of his illustration depicts the view of Lickskillet looking west from the Missouri side of the Missouri River, and was based on a photograph of an actual duck blind and decoy layout. It shows the old Cathedral of the Immaculate Conception, the grain silos, the waterworks intake building, and the two big anchor trees to the left of the intake building.

My editor for this book, Mr. Tom Turkle, was suggested to me by my mentor and editor of my first book, *Lickskillet*, Mr. Johnny Johnston III, now deceased. Mr. Turkle was at one time a book publisher and for many years Mr. Johnston was his assistant. The transition was smooth, and I shall be eternally grateful for his teaching and his patience with me as I again tried my hand at writing.

The following have been helpful in my preparation of this book:

Randy and Sue Martin
Alfred Goetz
John Goetz
Charles Schaar
Annie Johnston
Roger Card
Tony Watson
Connie Ingersol Knight
John Bollin
U.S. Army Corps of Engineers

The Author

Julius Cord attended Immaculata High School in Leavenworth and the University of Kansas. He worked at Missouri Valley Steel in Leavenworth and served in the Army during the Korean War. He retired from National Steel, Inc., where he worked for twenty years. He is president of Cord Marketing, Inc., and now lives in Okemos, Michigan.

This book and Mr. Cord's first book, *Lickskillet*, may be ordered directly through the author:

Julius Cord
4453 Oaklawn Drive
Okemos, MI 48864-2921
E-mail: j597@aol.com